Shattered Wings

Aircraft Accidents of the Great Lakes Region

by
W. D. Becker

INLAND

EXPRESSIONS

Clinton Township, Michigan

Published by Inland Expressions

Inland Expressions
42211 Garfield Rd. #297
Clinton Township, MI. 48038

www.inlandexpressions.com

First Edition 2013

Copyright @ 2013 by Inland Expressions

The photographs and information contained within have been
researched thoroughly but while the author and publisher of this book
have made every effort to provide accurate information they are by no
means responsible for any errors or omissions to the publication.

It is recognized that some of the names and designations used within
this publication are the property of the trademark owner. In such cases,
they are used for identification purposes only.

ISBN-13 978-1-939150-04-2

Printed in the United States of America.

Design by Inland Expressions

Table of Contents

Preface

Today, some 110 years after the Wright Brothers conducted their first successful powered flight, air travel has grown to become the world's safest form of transportation. This enviable status, however, has come at a price as it was attained, in large part, by the exhaustive investigation of aircraft accidents.

With its large population and manufacturing centers, it was only natural that air travel through the Great Lakes region increased in proportion to the growth of the aviation industry during the twentieth century. In fact, for many years, two airports at Chicago, first Midway and later O'Hare, could boast of being the busiest airfield in the world. Therefore, it should come as no surprise that six of the accidents included in this book involve aircraft either en route to or having departed from that city.

By its very nature, the dangers of air travel are many. All of the crashes in the following chapters took place between 1928 and 1970. During this timeframe, the process of aircraft accident investigation matured immeasurably, a fact reflected in this book by the increasing sophistication of details available in later chapters compared to earlier ones. Likewise, as no photographs exist for a number of the following accidents described herein, and those that do show little but wreckage which, in the end, contributes little to the story, it was determined not include any such illustrations in this book.

A decision to include brief histories of the aircraft types involved in these accidents was made during the initial phase of this book's creation. The purpose of this was to provide the reader with an insight into the developmental history of these aircraft.

Several notable aircraft accidents have occurred in the Great Lakes region. Included in this book are the first crashes involving the Lockheed Model 10 Electra, and Boeing 727, as well as the first fatal crash of a Ford Tri-Motor.

The selection process of stories included in this book placed an emphasis upon incorporating a number of lesser-known aircraft accidents that have occurred in the Great Lakes region. As such, it is hoped that the reader will gain a new perspective of this area's unique aviation heritage.

Chapter One
Crash of the first "Tin Goose"

On June 11, 1926, the first Ford 4-AT Tri-Motor embarked upon its maiden flight at Dearborn, Michigan. Intended for research and development purposes to validate the design of Ford's new airliner, this aircraft originally featured an open cockpit. While tragedy lay hidden in the future for this prototype, when it left the ground for the first time on that summer day in 1926 it was truly king of the skies.

Becoming interested in the growing aviation market, Henry Ford had invested in the Stout Metal Airplane Company during the early 1920s, before acquiring the company outright in 1925. By this time, the automotive giant had established Ford Airport at Dearborn, Michigan, along with the Ford Air Transport Service, the first regularly scheduled commercial airline in the United States.[1] Among the innovations pioneered at Ford Field during the early years of its existence was the construction of a passenger terminal and the world's first concrete runways.

Much of the credit deserved for laying the groundwork towards the development of the Ford Tri-Motor belongs to William B. Stout. Possessing a lifelong interest in aviation, Stout was a gifted engineer. In 1922, he founded the Stout Metal Airplane Company at Dearborn. At the time Stout formed this company, fabric was the material of choice for covering an aircraft's structure. Requiring regular replacement, however, the maintenance cost of fabric accounted for a large percentage of an

1

aircraft's operating cost. Therefore, the extra expense of covering an aircraft with metal could be offset by the reducing its maintenance costs over its operational life. One of Stout's early designs was for a twin-engine all-metal torpedo bomber for the U.S. Navy. Designated as the ST-1, only one example of this aircraft was manufactured. The destruction of the prototype in a crash during government trials, however, prompted the cancellation of the project.

Somewhat more successful was the all-metal Stout 2-AT Air Pullman. Eleven examples of this single engine design were built, five of which began operations with the Ford Air Transport Service in 1925 on the Detroit to Chicago route. By the end of 1927, however, the introduction of the new ATC (Approved Type Certificate) licensing system led to the Air Pullman's withdrawal from service.[2]

As mentioned earlier, the Stout Metal Airplane Company became a division of the Ford Motor Company in 1925. Following this transaction, William Stout's role in the organization became focused upon the development of new designs, specifically a three-engine commercial transport, rather than the actual manufacture of aircraft.

Using the 2-AT as the basis for a three-engine design, William Stout developed the 3-AT. This aircraft was powered by three Wright J-4 Whirlwind engines, one of which was mounted in the nose, while the other two were positioned in the leading edge of the high-mounted wing. The pilot was seated in an open cockpit above the passenger cabin. First flying in November 1925, it soon became apparent that the aircraft's 60 mph landing speed was too fast for grass strips. Although Stout felt that concrete runways would solve this problem, Henry Ford supported the idea of lowering the aircraft's landing speed, thus necessitating a major redesign effort.[3]

Furthermore, having promoted the 3-AT as the "airplane of the future," Ford was deeply disappointed with the aircraft's sluggish performance and saw to it that Stout was reassigned away from the engineering department. Replacing Stout as chief engineer was Harold Hicks, whom along with Thomas Towle shouldered the burden of formulating a new design.

During the early morning hours of January 17, 1926, a fire destroyed the Stout Metal Airplane factory at Ford Field. This loss, estimated at $500,000 in 1926, included the destruction of 13 Wright Whirlwind engines, a 2-AT Air Pullman used by the Postal Service, and the 3-AT prototype.[4]

From the ashes, a new design, the 4-AT, emerged within the next few months. The 4-AT bore a remarkable resemblance to the Fokker F.VII, a Dutch aircraft that had first flown in 1924. Designed with an open cockpit, the Ford 4-AT-A Tri-Motor could carry up to eight passengers.[5] Design and construction work on the Ford Tri-Motor progressed quickly through the first half of 1926, with the prototype being ready for its first flight by early June of that year.

Powered by three 200 horsepower Wright J-4 Whirlwind engines, the prototype took to the skies on June 11, 1926.[6] Overall, the 4-AT embodied a much more graceful and practical design than that of the ungainly 3-AT. Compared to the previous aircraft, among the most notable differences with the new design was the placement of the cockpit at the level of the passenger cabin, and the mounting of two of the aircraft's

The eight 4-AT Tri-Motors acquired by the United States Army Air Corps (USAAC) between 1928 and 1929 were assigned the C-3 designation. (USAF)

engines on metal struts underneath the high-mounted wing.

With a wingspan of 74 feet, a length of 50 feet, and a height of 12 feet, the 4-AT Tri-Motor had a gross takeoff weight of 10,130 pounds. The skin of the aircraft was made of corrugated aluminum, a material that provided great strength, but at the cost of poor aerodynamic performance. Regardless, the Ford 4-AT Tri-Motor, or "Tin Goose" as it became more popularly known, had a cruising speed of 83 knots (95 mph), and a range of just over 500 miles. While the 4-AT-A variant of the Tri-Motor could seat up to eight passengers, subsequent versions featuring increased wingspans and more powerful engines were capable of carrying nearly twice as many passengers. Interestingly, all of the control cables for the aircraft's movable surfaces were mounted externally on the fuselage.

4

After completing its duties as a research and development platform, the prototype 4-AT-A entered service for the Ford Air Transport Service following a rebuild that included enclosing the cockpit. The passage of the Air Commerce Act of 1926 established the Aeronautics Branch of the Department of Commerce.[7] A primary responsibility of this organization was the licensing of all aircraft and pilots in the United States. As such, Temporary Number 2435 was issued by the bureau to the first 4-AT-A Tri-Motor in May of 1927, before a permanent registration, NC-1492, was assigned five months later.[8]

By the morning of May 12, 1928, NC-1492 had logged some 100,000 miles in the service of the Ford Air Transport Service. On that date, this aircraft was being loaded at the Ford Airport with 1,200 pounds of freight destined for Buffalo, New York. The pilots assigned to fly the aircraft on this flight were William Munn and Earl Parker. Living in Detroit, both of these pilots had been recently hired by the company.

While this would be his first flight over a regular Ford Air Transport route, William Munn had previous experience as a test pilot for the Hess Aircraft Company of Wyandotte, Michigan. Prior to arriving in Michigan, Earl Parker had resided in Denver, Colorado. Both men were married.[9]

With the cargo loaded, the two pilots started up the aircraft's three engines and began taxiing to the runway in preparation for departure. At 8:45 a.m., with all final checks completed, the cargo plane began rolling down the runway. Shortly after rising into the air, however, the aircraft entered into a stall. As the Tri-Motor lost lift, it began rolling to the left. With its left wing dipping towards the ground, the aircraft began an uncontrolled

5

descent.

A few moments later, the left wing struck the ground near the Michigan Central Railroad tracks just outside of the airport. Spinning into the ground, a fuel tank was ruptured and the aircraft burst into flames, killing both Munn and Parker instantly. After battling the blaze for over an hour, rescue crews were finally able to retrieve the bodies of the unfortunate crewmen.

This crash represented the first fatal accident involving a Ford Tri-Motor. Interviewed by reporters shortly after the accident, Edward G. Hamilton, chief of operations for the Ford Air Transport Service, stated that the accident occurred due to the pilot forcing the plane into the air before gaining a speed sufficient for flight.[10]

The fuselage of the Ford Tri-Motor was completely covered with corrugated aluminum, a design feature that provided great strength at the cost of aerodynamic performance. (USAF)

The crash of NC-1492 was the third serious accident to occur at the Ford Airport between April and May 1928. On April 24 of that year, two aviators from New York were killed when their Taylor monoplane crashed from an altitude of 1,000 feet during a demonstration flight. One day prior to this accident, three people were injured in another crash at the airport.[11]

Manufacture of the Ford Tri-Motor continued until June 1933, by which time 199 examples of this aircraft had been produced. While most of these aircraft were placed into service with commercial airlines such as TWA and United, some found their way into military service. During the late 1920s, the U.S. Army Air Corps (USAAC) acquired eight examples of the 4-AT Tri-Motor, consisting of one 4-AT-A and seven 4-AT-Es, which were redesignated as the C-3 and C-3A respectively.[12] Perhaps the most unique role in which the Ford Tri-Motor served was its use as an aerobatic aircraft for air show performances. During these displays, pilots often demonstrated the three-engine aircraft's ability to perform spins and loops, an amazing sight considering the size of the aircraft.

After years of losing money, and with the Great Depression in full swing, the Ford Motor Company shut down its aircraft division in 1936. Although it ceased building airplanes of its own design, the company later manufactured over 8,600 B-24 Liberator Bombers at its Willow Run plant during World War II. Closed in 1947, the property on which Ford Airport once occupied is serving today as the site of Ford's Dearborn Proving Grounds.

Although the last example of the Ford Tri-Motor left the factory eighty years ago, at least eighteen of these aircraft remain in existence. Representing nearly ten percent of the total built, this number is more remarkable when considering that the aircraft was outclassed in terms of performance within a few years of entering operational service. Attesting to the type's dependability and toughness, a number of Tri-Motors provided years of service as bush planes in the far reaches of Alaska. As of 2012, eight Ford Tri-Motors remain airworthy, some of which make annual appearances around the country on the air show circuit.

Chapter Two
Rushed into Service

Reeling from the economic impact of the Great Depression, the Detroit Aircraft Corporation went into receivership during the fall of 1931. The following year, a group of investors, headed by Robert E. Gross, acquired the Lockheed Aircraft Company from the bankrupt airplane manufacturer for $40,000 ($670,000 in 2012 dollars). Shortly afterwards, Gross began planning the development of an all-metal, single-engine airliner capable of carrying ten passengers. Before work began, however, market research pointed out that a twin-engine design would be more attractive to the airlines.[1] Utilizing this information as a basis for their decision, Lockheed's management chose to adopt a twin-engine, low-wing design for the new aircraft, which was designated as the Model 10 Electra.

The primary responsibility for the design of Lockheed's first all-metal aircraft fell upon Hall L. Hibbard, its chief engineer. During wind tunnel testing conducted at the University of Michigan, a professor assistant by the name of Clarence "Kelly" Johnson became involved with the Electra. Johnson, who subsequently joined Lockheed and oversaw the development of some of that company's most unique and famous aircraft, made a number of suggestions concerning the Electra's airframe. While several of Johnson's ideas were incorporated into the aircraft's final design, perhaps the most notable was the substitution of the original conventional tail with twin fins and rudders, a feature that figured prominently in several subsequent Lockheed aircraft, including the infamous Constellation.

The first flight of a Model 10 Electra took place on February 23, 1934. Lockheed received such an enthusiastic response from the airlines that by the middle of that same year it could boast of accepting orders for twenty-two examples of its short-range airliner.[2] In October 1934, the decision to adopt a twin-engine design bore fruit when the U.S. Government prohibited the operation of single-engine passenger carrying aircraft during night or over rough terrain. As such, Lockheed was in a favorable position to pick up additional orders from the airlines.[3]

Powered by two 450 horsepower Pratt & Whitney R-985 Wasp Junior radial engines, the Model 10-A Electra had a cruising speed of 169 knots (195 mph) at an altitude of 9,600 feet. Flown by a crew of two, this aircraft was capable of carrying up to ten passengers in its simple, but functional, passenger cabin over a range of 810 miles. With a wingspan of 55 feet, the Electra had a wing area equal to 458 square feet. While the airliner's tail wheel was not retractable, the two main landing gear struts retracted into positions behind the engines that left their wheels partially exposed.

Among the early air carriers placing orders for the Electra were Northwest Airlines and Pan American Airways, the former of which became the first to put the aircraft into service. Late in the summer of 1934, Lockheed delivered one of the earliest examples off the production line to Northwest. Licensed as NC-14243 by the Department of Commerce, the airline wasted little time in placing this aircraft into scheduled service.

On the evening of August 7, 1934, the crew of NC-14243 was preparing to depart from St. Paul, Minnesota on a flight destined for Chicago, Illinois with intermediate stops at Minneapolis and Milwaukee. The crew conducting this flight consisted of 34-year-old Captain Joseph Ohrbeck and his 20-year-old copilot, John Woodhead, both of whom lived in St. Paul.

While preparing NC-14243 for the evening flight to Chicago, ground crews filled both of the aircraft's 100-gallon tanks with a full load of fuel. Shortly after 9:00 p.m., even as the darkening summer skies overhead continued the transition from twilight to nighttime, the airliner's two radial engines came to life.[4] Satisfied all was in order, Captain Ohrbeck began taxiing his 10,000-pound aircraft to the runway.

Lining up on the runway at 9:25 p.m., nearly an hour and a half past the flight's originally scheduled departure time, Captain

An early photograph of a Lockheed Model 10 Electra showing the type's original forward-raked windscreen. (Author's Collection)

Ohrbeck pushed the throttles controlling the aircraft's engines forward to begin the takeoff roll. As the engines responded, the brand new airliner began moving down the runway. A few seconds later, as the Electra continued to accelerate, its tail lifted off the ground. Thundering down the runway, while picking up even more speed, the lift generated by the wings finally overcame the force of gravity and the Northwest airliner climbed into the sky. This entire process had taken less than one minute to accomplish.

A few minutes after departing St. Paul, the 10-seat airliner arrived at nearby Minneapolis. Following a brief stop, NC-14243 rose once again above the landscape of southern Minnesota. Turning onto a westerly course that would take it over the farmlands of Wisconsin to the shores of Lake Michigan, the airliner began its 300-mile trek towards Milwaukee. At 11:45 p.m., following an uneventful flight, the Electra touched down at the Milwaukee County Airport.

While preparing to depart St. Paul, Captain Ohrbeck had placed the aircraft's fuel selector valve into a position that allowed the engines to consume fuel from both tanks simultaneously. About 1¼ hours into the flight, however, he noticed the fuel gauge for the left tank read that it was still full, while the right tank was registering that it was only ⅝ full. Attempting to correct this discrepancy, Ohrbeck changed the valve switch to drain fuel from the left tank only, a configuration in which the Electra was flown until landing at Milwaukee an hour later.[5]

Upon landing at Milwaukee, the crew of the Electra noticed that the fuel gauge for the left tank was indicating that it was only ½ full. Meanwhile, the reading for the right tank had remained unchanged since the fuel selector switch had been set to drain fuel from the left tank only. In addition to not taking on any additional fuel at Milwaukee, the pilots made no further changes to the aircraft's fuel system prior to departure.

As midnight approached, Captain Ohrbeck turned the small airliner onto the runway to perform his third takeoff of the evening. In addition to the two pilots, seven other persons were aboard NC-14243 as it prepared to depart Milwaukee for the short flight to Chicago. Those purchasing tickets for this flight came from across the United States, and included Arthur G. Callahan, Munising, Michigan; Dr. William R. P. Clark, San Francisco, California; Donald Couture, Duluth, Minnesota; Frank Cooper, Wenatchee, Washington; Lester Edge, Spokane, Washington; and George Merkes, Old Forge, New York. Joining this group of passengers in the cabin was Manfred G. Boe, a Northwest Airlines instrument expert from Minneapolis.[6] Also loaded aboard the aircraft, by special request, was a pouch of mail belonging to the U.S. Postal Service.

At 11:56 p.m., the Northwest Airlines Electra began advancing down the runway at the Milwaukee County Airport. Using fuel from the left tank only, the takeoff proceeded normally until the aircraft had risen barely twenty feet above the ground. At this point, the left engine suddenly quit, this being accompanied by the nearly simultaneous activation of the fuel warning lights in the cockpit. Reacting immediately, Ohrbeck changed the fuel selector switch to feed fuel from both tanks, while Copilot Woodhead attempted to get fuel to the left engine by using the plane's wobble pump.[7]

13

Dropping from the sky, the Electra stuck the ground with sufficient force to destroy the right tire and its associated landing gear structure. Even as this occurred, the left engine coughed back to life, which, in conjunction with the still operational right engine, forced the airliner to bounce back into the air. After ascending to approximately seventy-five feet in height, the right engine stopped running as it ran out of fuel. With the left engine still operating, this caused the airliner to make a slight turn to the right. Captain Ohrbeck responded by switching the fuel selector valve back to the left tank. Alongside the Northwest Airlines captain, John Woodhead continued his unsuccessful struggle to get fuel to flow by desperately working the wobble pump by hand.

As NC-14243 began settling back to earth, its left engine lost power once again. Banking to the right and descending in a nose -down attitude, the doomed aircraft just narrowly missed hitting a house before crashing into a marshy area just outside the airport. Tumbling across the wet ground for nearly seventy-five feet, the wrecked airliner finally came to rest in an upright position. Although the darkness of the night prevented personnel at the Milwaukee County Airport from witnessing the crash, the sound of the impact was clearly heard.[8] Arriving at the scene, rescuers found that several of the passengers had been thrown from the aircraft as it broke apart. Strewn all about the mangled wreckage were pieces of the passenger's baggage and the contents of the mail shipment.

Although no lives were lost in the crash, everyone aboard the airliner was injured when it ploughed into the ground. These injuries ranged from minor to severe in nature. The most

The USAAC acquired the Model 10 Electra under the C-36 designation. This example illustrates the revised windscreen design. (USAF)

seriously injured included Dr. William R. P. Clark, Frank Cooper, Donald Couture, and Captain Ohrbeck. With the exception of Frank Cooper, whom had sustained serious back injuries, each of these individuals had suffered brain concussions in the accident. Meanwhile, the remainder of those aboard the airliner requiring medical treatment suffered injuries of a minor nature, these amounting mostly to abrasions, lacerations, and bruises.[9]

The responsibility to investigate the crash of NC-14243 fell upon the Bureau of Air Commerce, the aeronautics branch of the Department of Commerce. During this investigation, it was found that Northwest Airlines had placed this aircraft into service almost immediately after receiving it from the manufacturer. Among other things, such a practice did not allow time for company personnel to establish any working knowledge of the aircraft's hourly fuel consumption rate.[10]

This operating deficiency was compounded by the fact that this was Captain Ohrbeck's first flight in this particular aircraft. Investigators were able to establish that the Northwest captain was operating the airliner based on the assumption that it burned fuel at a rate of approximately 43 gallons per hour. Such a consumption rate would have generally agreed with the fuel tank level readings taken upon landing at Milwaukee. Such a presumption, however, could not explain the discrepancy observed by the pilots 1¼ hours into the flight when the right tank registered that it was only ⅝ full while the left tank continued indicating that it remained full, despite the fact that both tanks should have been draining equally since taking off from St. Paul.

In spite of the left tank's fuel gauge showing that it still contained ½ of its load of fuel at the time of the crash, an investigation of NC-14243's fuel system revealed that, in actuality, only about one gallon of fuel remained in this tank. A similar examination of the right tank, however, found that it still held between fifty and sixty gallons of fuel, which translated very closely with the ⅝ full reading on its fuel gauge prior to the takeoff off from Milwaukee. Using these values, investigators estimated that the aircraft's actual rate of fuel consumption amounted to approximately 60 gallons per hour, a figure significantly higher than that estimated by Captain Ohrbeck.

The Bureau of Air Commerce issued its final report concerning this accident on January 9, 1935. In this narrative, Northwest Airlines was criticized for failing to formulate the aircraft's actual fuel consumption characteristics prior to placing it into service. Although, the Accident Board cited the left tank's defective fuel gauge as a contributing factor, it also disapproved of Captain

Ohrbeck's failure to utilize the right fuel tank after receiving a warning on his instrument panel that the tank he had selected was practically empty.

Occurring within four days of being awarded its Approved Type Certificate, the loss of NC-14243 represented the first crash involving a Lockheed Model 10 Electra. Between August 1934 and July 18, 1941, a total of 149 Electras came off the assembly line.[11] Built in four major variants, these aircraft found service with both civilian and military operators around the world. Perhaps the most famous of all Electras was a Model 10-E flown by Amelia Earhart when she disappeared over the central Pacific Ocean on July 2, 1937. While a few of these impressive aircraft remain in existence today, the vast majority of Electras built were withdrawn from service by the late 1970s.

Nearly twenty years after the first flight of its pioneering twin-engine airliner, the name Electra was to play another part in the history of the Lockheed Aircraft Corporation. During the mid-1950s, Lockheed applied the same name to its Model 188 (L-188) turboprop airliner design. Failing to sell in large numbers to the airlines, the L-188 Electra was subsequently used as the basis for the far more successful P-3 Orion anti-submarine patrol aircraft.

Chapter Three
"Quite a jolt..."

On the afternoon of December 17, 1935, exactly thirty-two years to the day of the Wright Brother's first powered flight, the prototype Douglas DC-3 embarked upon its maiden flight.[1] First ordered by American Airlines during mid-1935, this aircraft was an enlarged version of its immediate predecessor, the DC-2.

Superior to other passenger aircraft available at the time, the DC-3 revolutionized commercial aviation not only in the United States, but around the world as well. Even as American Airlines conducted their first revenue flight with the DC-3 on July 11, 1936, the Douglas Aircraft Company was being flooded with orders for their new plane from other carriers. Within three years, the DC-3 was operating for a number of airlines throughout the United States, including Braniff, Eastern, Transcontinental & Western (TWA), and United.[2] Joining the list of early air carriers placing the DC-3 into service was Pennsylvania Central Airlines (PCA), which later became Capital Airlines, the operator of the aircraft involved in this chapter's accident.

By the onset of the World War II, the DC-3 was well established in operations around the globe. The aircraft's potential was not to be lost to the U.S. military. In September 1940, the U.S. Army Air Corps placed its first order with Douglas for the C-47 Skytrain, a version of the DC-3 adapted for military use. Seeing action in every theater of the Second World War, over 10,000 examples of this aircraft were to be manufactured throughout the duration of the conflict.

The C-47 was produced in a wide array of variants during the war, including the C-53D Skytrooper. Optimized for carrying paratroopers and towing gliders, this model lacked the reinforced floor and double doors found on the C-47.

With an empty weight of 18,200 pounds, the C-53D Skytrooper had a length of 63 feet 9 inches. Each of this aircraft's two Pratt & Whitney R-1830 radial engines was capable of generating 1,200 horsepower, giving the transport a top speed of 230 mph. Stretching 95 feet 6 inches, the wingspan of the C-53D was nearly 50 percent longer than its fuselage.

The entire production run of the C-53D totaled 159 examples, one of which bore the serial number 42-68849. Shortly after

A C-53D Skytrooper. (USAF)

conducting its first flight in 1943, this aircraft was placed into service with the U.S. Army Air Forces (USAAF).

When the war ended in 1945, the USAAF possessed a gigantic fleet of transport aircraft, a number much larger than could be economically maintained during peacetime. Therefore, when the military demobilized, a large number of these aircraft were acquired by civil operators for use in the growing commercial market.

Purchased by Capital Airlines on December 15, 1945, 42-68849 was reregistered as NC-45379. Converted to the DC-3A specification, this aircraft soon entered service on Capital's extensive network of routes throughout the eastern United States. Since its introduction, the DC-3 had earned a reputation as being a rugged aircraft, a characteristic that would play a major role in the history of NC-45379.

On the afternoon of August 7, 1949, Capital Airlines' Flight 19 arrived at Detroit, Michigan on one of its scheduled stops between Norfolk, Virginia and Milwaukee, Wisconsin. While at Detroit, a routine crew change took place. Coming aboard NC-45379 to take command was 29 year-old, Captain Jack N. Bolick of Detroit. Bolick had been with Capital Airlines since being hired on June 17, 1942. With 5,146 flight hours aboard DC-3 type aircraft, and having flown on this particular route since 1943, Bolick was superbly qualified to command Flight 19.

Joining Captain Bolick in the cockpit was First Officer L. F. Davis, age 32, whom had worked for Capital since April 29, 1946. Davis had amassed 6,826 flight hours, 942 of which were with the DC-3. Rounding out the aircraft's crew, and attending to the various needs of the passengers, was Stewardess Shirley

Davidson of Coldwater, Michigan.[3]

After its departure from Detroit, the Capital Airlines DC-3 headed towards Muskegon, Michigan, on the eastern shore of Lake Michigan. Following an uneventful trip, NC-45379, with 20 passengers aboard, departed that city at 4:34 p.m. bound for General Mitchell Field, just outside of Milwaukee.[4] Cleared to proceed the 80 miles across the freshwater lake via a visual flight rules (VFR) flight plan, the crew of the airliner pointed their craft west to complete the last leg of its scheduled route from Norfolk.[5]

With clear skies and fifteen miles visibility, the weather on this segment of the trip was nearly perfect. This eased the workload faced by the crew of the 23,000 pound aircraft while operating under VFR conditions. Such favorable weather also provided the passengers in the cabin with a wonderful view of the blue waters of Lake Michigan as their airliner cruised 4,000 feet above the waves.

As the Capital Airlines DC-3 continued its journey towards Milwaukee, Arthur Rapps, a bus driver from that city, was preparing to depart Maitland Field in a Cessna 140.[6] Possessing a private pilot's license, Rapps, age 33, had approximately 225 flight hours in light aircraft and was co-owner of the Cessna 140, serial number N-3198N.

Located on the lakefront, and bordered on three sides by the city of Milwaukee, Maitland Field had only one runway, which was aligned in a north and south direction. Due to the runway's orientation, pilots departing this airfield typically entered a traffic pattern to gain altitude before departing the area. This allowed aircraft operating from the small airport to avoid flying

A DC-3 operated by Capital Airlines similar to the aircraft involved in the accident related in this chapter. (Author's Collection)

over the city at low altitude. On this particular afternoon, landings were being made to the south, therefore a left hand traffic pattern was in use, which pilots were to enter or leave at an altitude of 800 feet.[7]

About six miles out of Milwaukee, the crew of the Capital Airlines' DC-3 contacted the control tower at General Mitchell Field. After being advised that the wind was from south-southeast, at eight to ten miles per hour, and that runway 13 was in use, the propeller-driven airliner began its descent from 4,000 feet at a speed of 160 miles per hour.

At approximately 5:00 p.m., Arthur Rapps departed Maitland Field in his Cessna 140. Having flown the light plane out of this airfield since March of that year, Rapps was familiar with the airport's traffic pattern and thus began circling the airport in a series of left hand turns as he gained altitude.

Their prelanding checklist completed, Captain Bolick and First Officer Davis aboard the DC-3 maintained a constant lookout for any air traffic as they approached the Wisconsin shoreline on a heading of 270 degrees. Although a number of light aircraft were observed operating in the vicinity, none was considered to pose a danger to the airliner.

As the Capital Airlines DC-3 flew over Maitland Field, it began a shallow left turn to a heading of 225 degrees. At the same moment, Arthur Rapps in N-3198N was observed making a left turn over the southwest boundary of the airfield as he continued his climb. The two aircraft were now on a collision course over downtown Milwaukee.

At 5:09 p.m., in what Captain Bolick later described as "quite a jolt," the right wing of the DC-3 collided with the Cessna 140. The collision tore off approximately 6 feet of the airliner's right wingtip as well as severing the right aileron near its fourth hinge point away from the fuselage. While the force of the collision damaged the Cessna's undercarriage and bent its left rear wing strut outwards, its fuselage, engine, wings, and tail section remained intact.[8] After being brushed aside by the much larger DC-3, however, the light plane began spiraling towards the ground. A few seconds later, the small craft crashed into a parking lot, killing Arthur Rapps instantly.

Standing in the aisle when the accident occurred, Stewardess Shirley Davidson felt the impact, but initially had no idea as to what had just taken place, a feeling she shared with the plane's passengers. This changed quickly, however, as the DC-3's heavily damaged wing was clearly visible through the windows on the right hand side of the cabin. In spite of the damage inflicted by the collision, the airliner continued flying in a stable manner, thus panic did not break out amongst the twenty passengers.[9]

With its controls working within normal parameters, Captain Bolick brought the wounded DC-3 into General Mitchell Field for a safe landing. With the exception of the fatal injuries suffered by Arthur Rapps in the Cessna, no one aboard the DC-3, or on the ground, was injured.

The wreckage of the Cessna 140, along with the aileron section and wingtip of the DC-3, came to rest approximately 360 feet southwest of the Maitland Field. Striking the ground at a nearly vertical nose down attitude, the engine and propeller of the small plane were found deeply embedded in the ground. It was discovered that the Cessna's right wheel was severed from the aircraft at the time of the collision, this component being found some 2,500 feet west of Maitland Field.[10]

The Civil Aeronautics Board (CAB) received notification of this accident at 6:35 p.m. (CST) on August 7, 1949, and as required by regulations, initiated an investigation. At one point during the probe, investigators conducted a series of test flights over the actual site of the accident with Captain Bolick at the controls of a DC-3 belonging to the CAB. This was done as part of an effort to reconcile the aircraft's actual altitude at the time of the collision with the observations of witnesses on the ground.

During its review, the accident investigation board determined that the Cessna was conducting a climbing left turn and was ahead and to the right of the DC-3. While executing such a maneuver, the oncoming airliner would have been invisible to the light plane's pilot, as it would have been obstructed by the left side of the overhead mounted wing.

The findings of the Civil Aeronautics Board investigation were released on March 28, 1950. The investigators concluded that the accident was caused by the failure of the pilots aboard the Capital Airlines' DC-3 to observe and avoid the Cessna 140.

Following extensive repairs, NC-45379 returned to service with Capital Airlines. This aircraft remained operational for nearly another 37 years, before crashing at San Juan, Puerto Rico on July 22, 1986, killing one of the two pilots aboard. At the time of this accident, the DC-3 was operating for Borinquen Air, a small charter airline based in Puerto Rico, and registered as N27PR.[11]

Following many years of declining use, Maitland Field ceased operations during the mid- 1950s. In 1956, the U.S. Army selected the site for the basing of Nike air defense missiles. It continued to be used in this role until the threat posed by Soviet bombers receded during the late 1960s. Today, the property on which Maitland Field once stood is known as the Henry W. Maier Festival Park, or the Summerfest Grounds, the location of the world's largest annual music festival.

Currently, several examples of the DC-3, and its many derivatives, remain in operational service around the world. This aircraft has earned a well-deserved reputation as being one of the most famous aircraft in the history of aviation. Most likely, it will also become one of the longest serving aircraft types, as it is highly probable that a number of these amazing craft will still be airworthy in 2035, when the one-hundred year anniversary of its first flight is celebrated.

Chapter Four
A Troubled Design

The morning of October 13, 1950 began as quietly as most others for the small community of Almelund, Minnesota. Located just a few miles west of the Wisconsin border, in Chisago County, those living in this area were going about their regular business that particular Friday morning oblivious to the life and death struggle taking place in the clear blue skies overhead. It is nearly 11 a.m. on that peaceful morning when the pilots of a Martin 2-0-2 passenger plane belonging to Northwest Airlines lost the struggle to regain control of their doomed airliner, thus shattering the calm surroundings of the tiny farming community.

In November 1945, the Glenn L. Martin Company of Baltimore, Maryland, announced plans to manufacture a twin-engine passenger airliner capable of carrying up to 40 passengers. Designated as the Model 2-0-2, the new design offered a significant increase in performance over that of the Douglas DC-3 and Curtiss C-46, two prewar designs then in service with a number of domestic airlines. The sales department at Martin succeeded in obtaining a number of significant orders from Eastern, Northwest, Pennsylvania-Central (later Capital Airlines), Colonial, and TWA.[1] In spite of these early marketing successes, however, subsequent events prompted the cancellation of a significant portion of these orders.

The first flight of a Martin 2-0-2 occurred on November 22, 1946. This aircraft was followed into the air by a second prototype, while a third airframe was constructed for static testing purposes. On August 13, 1947, the Martin 2-0-2 became the first postwar designed twin-engine airliner to receive a Civil Aeronautics Administration (CAA) type operating certificate.[2]

Measuring 71 feet 4 inches in length, the 2-0-2 had a wingspan of 93 feet 3 inches. The wings featured a considerable dihedral (upward) angle and large double slotted flaps. Flown by a crew of two or three, this aircraft could accommodate up to forty passengers in its unpressurized cabin. To facilitate the aircraft's turnaround capabilities during short stops, a ventral staircase was installed in the passenger cabin that permitted passengers to embark and disembark below the tail while the engines remained at ground idle.

Powered by a pair of 2,400 hp Pratt & Whitney R-2800-CA18 Double Wasp engines, the Martin 2-0-2 had a maximum cruising speed of 240 knots (276 mph). These engines were the same that powered this aircraft's direct competitor, the Convair 240. Nearly identical in appearance, the prototype of Convair's twin-engine airliner first flew on March 16, 1947 and entered series production later that year.

The Martin 2-0-2 first entered revenue service with LAN-Chile in October 1947, this being followed by Northwest Airlines inaugurating domestic service the following month.[3] By this time, Eastern had delayed its order for the 2-0-2 after finding the Martin Company reluctant to accept a number of design changes it had requested. Meanwhile, TWA postponed its purchase of the aircraft due to financial constraints. Although appreciable, the problems facing Martin concerning Eastern's changing requirements and the general collapse of the commercial market

One of the Martin 2-0-2 prototypes in its manufacturer's markings. (Author's Collection)

during 1947 was to be pale in comparison to what was to come.

On August 29, 1948, a Northwest Martin 2-0-2, registered as NC93044, crashed after encountering a thunderstorm near Winona, Minnesota, killing 37. An investigation into this accident uncovered a structural weakness in the 2-0-2's wing. The discovery of this design flaw prompted the temporary grounding of all Martin 2-0-2s in service until modifications could be completed to prevent a similar accident.

In the end, only 47 Martin 2-0-2s were built, 25 of which were acquired by Northwest Airlines, thus making that carrier the major user of the type. One of these aircraft was purchased from the Glenn L. Martin Company on August 2, 1947. Headquartered at St. Paul, Minnesota, Northwest soon placed this airliner, now registered as NC93037, into service on its extensive network of routes spanning the northern region of the United States.

On the morning of October 13, 1950, NC93037 sat quietly at the

Minneapolis-St. Paul International Airport as ground crews prepared it for a local flight. Rather than carrying any paying passengers, the purpose of this particular flight was to conduct a six-month instrument competency check of Captain John R. Galt.

Employed by Northwest Airlines on December 5, 1939, Captain Galt was 38 years old and had logged a total of 9,800 flying hours during his career. Having received his initial certification to operate the Martin 2-0-2 on October 22, 1947, Galt had earned 769 flying hours operating this type of aircraft.

Supervising the competency check of Captain Galt was Captain Ray Render, a 38 year-old Northwest Airlines check pilot. Joining the air carrier on January 2, 1942, Render had amassed 8,228 flight hours during his career. On December 1, 1949, he completed his primary training on the Martin 2-0-2, and by the time of this flight had recorded 368 hours aboard the piston-powered airliner. Both Northwest captains lived in the Minneapolis-St. Paul area.

Also boarding the airliner on this fateful day were four observers from the Civil Aeronautics Administration (CAA), one of whom was William H. Solomon. Acting in his capacity as a CAA air carrier agent, Mr. Solomon occupied the jump seat immediately between and behind the two pilots in the cockpit. The other three observers were all personnel from the control tower at the Minneapolis-St. Paul Airport. Seated in the passenger cabin, this group included Everett C. Bergstrom, Bruce D. Erickson, and Robert H. Olsen.

Loaded with 800 gallons of fuel, NC93037 weighed 32,943 pounds when it began rolling down the runway at 9:46 a.m., to begin its final flight.[4] This was well below the aircraft's maximum allowable weight limit of 38,000 pounds. With clear skies and unlimited visibility, the aircraft's crew could not have asked for any more favorable weather conditions in which to conduct this assessment flight.

Following takeoff, the crew conducted two simulated ILS (instrument landing system) approaches at the airport. At the conclusion of the second approach, the crew informed the tower that they had completed this phase of the flight. Received at 10:25 a.m., this message later proved to be the final radio transmission received from the doomed airliner.

After leaving the Minneapolis area, the next sighting of NC93037 was made some 43 miles northeast of the airport at Center City, Minnesota. Here a witness reported seeing the Northwest airliner conducting a steep left turn at an altitude estimated as being between 4,000 and 5,000 feet. It was also noted that the aircraft's landing gear was down, and after the completion of this turn, the craft began a shallow climb. A few moments later, the same witness reported seeing the airliner in a partially inverted position as it entered into a steep dive. Before a successful recovery and return to level flight was performed by the crew, the observer estimated that the aircraft had descended approximately 2,500 feet, or at least half of the aircraft's original altitude when first sighted.

After returning to level flight, the aircraft began to head away in a northeasterly direction. A few moments later, it was observed making two or three oscillations about its lateral axis. During each of these maneuvers, which were accompanied by a noise characteristic of a surge in engine power, the airliner lost about 400 feet in altitude.[5]

The next sighting of the struggling aircraft took place at a location approximately five miles northeast of Center City and two miles south of Almelund, Minnesota. Here NC93037 was observed making a shallow right turn of approximately 270 degrees before returning to a level attitude on a northwesterly heading. A few moments later, at approximately 10:49 a.m., the airliner entered into a sharp right turn at approximately 500 to 600 feet above the ground. It was during this maneuver, that the twin-engine aircraft began rapidly losing what little altitude it had remaining.

After completing about 90 degrees of the right turn, the right wing of the Martin 2-0-2 struck the ground. As the force of the impact began tearing apart the wing, the aircraft rotated on its nose and slid a distance of 378 feet in an easterly direction. During the aircraft's breakup sequence, the fuselage was ripped into three major sections. One of the fuselage breaks occurred just in front of the leading edge of the wing, the other just aft of the wing's trailing edge.

During its skid along the ground, the airliner narrowly missed a pair of houses, in which four people were present. In one of the homes was Mrs. Eva Lundquist, and her granddaughter, Mrs. Arnie Selmans, while the other was occupied by Mr. and Mrs. Victor Selmans, an elderly couple.[6]

Although rescuers successfully pulled Bruce D. Erickson from the shattered remains of the wrecked airliner, they soon ascertained that all of the other five persons aboard had perished in the accident. Suffering from a skull fracture, compound leg fracture, and severe shock, Erickson was in critical condition when he was taken to a hospital in nearby St. Croix Falls,

Wisconsin.[7] Several days later, however, the CAA employee succumbed to his injuries without ever regaining consciousness.[8]

After being notified of the loss of NC93037, the Civil Aeronautics Board (CAB) launched an immediate investigation into the accident. Sifting through the wreckage, investigators were able to establish that there was no evidence that the aircraft had suffered a pre-crash fire or structural failure. Although the landing gear was found to be in the lowered position, it could not be positively established whether it was "locked." It was determined, however, that the wing flaps were in their fully retracted positions.

Although torn from their nacelles on the wings, both engines, and their respective propeller components, were recovered from the crash site. A teardown of the left engine revealed no evidence of any mechanical failure. Furthermore, the hydraulic, electrical, and mechanical systems of the left propeller were also found to be in working order.

When investigators performed a teardown examination of the right engine, however, it was found that although the powerplant had experienced an overspeed at some point, it was developing little, if any, power when the aircraft struck the ground. This finding supported the statements of witnesses that reported the airliner's right propeller spinning very slowly during the final moments before the crash.

When tested, the fuel feed valve on this engine was found unable to maintain its normal 10 psi (pounds per square inch) operating pressure. This indicated that the valve was being held off its seat, a diagnosis confirmed when a small particle of phenolic resin was found near the valve seat when this unit was disassembled.[9] This particle was deemed sufficient in size to cause the valve to stick open if it became lodged in the valve seat, or any other critical place within the valve mechanism. In such an instance, the resulting unbalanced pressure in the carburetor would eventually lead to an engine failure. Whether the particle of resin had dislodged prior to or as a result of the accident could not be determined.

An examination of the right propeller revealed that only a portion of the number one propeller blade remained attached to the hub. After this blade was removed from the hub, it was determined that the blades of this propeller were oriented 7 to 10 degrees in reverse pitch at the time of the crash. Tests conducted upon the feathering pump of this engine established that this unit was fully functional.

The cover plate of this propeller's governor solenoid valve was found damaged. Bench tests confirmed that the damaged cover plate allowed the solenoid valve to remain in a partially energized position. Subsequent testing confirmed that this condition could cause the blades of a propeller to move into the reverse angle pitch. Further testing, however, revealed that the solenoid's cover plate could not have been damaged prior to takeoff without the crew becoming aware of any unusual propeller responses. Furthermore, investigators could find no evidence that the right engine, nacelle, or solenoid valve had been struck by any object in flight.

In their quest to determine the reason for the propeller blades being in reverse pitch at the time of the accident, investigators began looking at the Martin 2-0-2's propeller electrical system. During this examination, it was found that an unwanted reversal of the propeller blades could occur under a number of conditions. The propeller electrical system of the accident aircraft, however, was so heavily damaged that it was impossible to determine whether any of these circumstances had occurred during the ill-fated flight.

During their probe, investigators were apprised of at least two other instances in which pilots operating Martin 2-0-2s had experienced an inadvertent propeller reversal. One of these took place during a test flight conducted by the aircraft's manufacturer. In this instance, the left propeller inadvertently reversed at an altitude of 3,500 feet and an airspeed of 113 knots (130 mph). After discovering he could not regain altitude lost during a descent to recover airspeed, the test pilot lowered the flaps and increased power on the right engine to METO (maximum except takeoff). In this configuration, the pilot was able to maintain an altitude of 1,500 feet and a airspeed of 104 knots (120 mph). Considering his control of the aircraft as being so marginal, the test pilot decided to perform a forced landing at a nearby small grass airfield rather than risk flying the 15 miles back to the Martin Airport.[10]

The second instance of an inadvertent propeller reversal involving a Martin 2-0-2 occurred while the aircraft was still on the ground. While performing his preflight checklist, the pilot of this aircraft pressed the feathering button to check the feathering system, which resulted in an engine overspeed and the propeller blades reorienting to their reverse thrust positions. Following several failed attempts by the pilot to rectify this situation, some maintenance work was performed on the aircraft after which the condition was not encountered again. Prompted by the crash of

NC93037, investigators reexamined this incident and concluded that the work done to the aircraft was inconsequential and that problem had actually been caused by an intermittent electrical short.

In the end, investigators were unable to determine at what point during the last flight of NC93037 that the right propeller blades went into the reverse thrust position. It is entirely possible that the propeller reversal brought upon the initial dive witnessed over Center City. Likewise, such a condition could have occurred after a recovery from the descent was accomplished. What is known, however, is that following this maneuver, the crew exhibited only minimal control over their aircraft. Compounding the complicated nature of the investigation was the lack of any messages transmitted by the crew concerning the difficulties they were encountering.

The resin particle found lodged in the right engine's fuel feed valve presented the possibility that the right engine lost power during the flight. In such a situation, proper procedure called for the pilots to feather the affected propeller to reduce drag, thus opening up the possibility that an electrical short in the propeller system may have caused an unwanted blade reversal. In the final analysis, however, investigators could not determine whether the resin particle became lodged in the feed valve before or as a result of the crash, and were therefore unable to establish its contribution, if any, to the accident.

The nature of the flight itself provided the investigation with another possible scenario for events leading up to the crash. It was considered plausible that a check of Captain Galt's competency on the Martin 2-0-2 may have included a validation of his single-engine procedures. If, as investigators theorized, there was a short in the aircraft's propeller electrical system, any intentional attempt to feather could have resulted in the right propeller entering a reverse thrust orientation.

Concluding a six-month investigation, the CAB issued their report concerning the crash of NC93037 on April 23, 1951. In this report, the Board issued the following statement concerning the probable cause of this crash:

> The Board determines that the probable cause of this accident was the unwanted reversal of the right propeller during flight, as a result of which the crew was unable to maintain control of the aircraft.

Following the Almelund crash, Northwest's troubled history with the Martin 2-0-2 continued. Over the next three months, the airline suffered two additional crashes involving this aircraft type, which resulted in the deaths of thirty-one people. Due in part of the growing reluctance of pilots to operate the type, Northwest began disposing of its Martin 2-0-2 fleet during the early months of 1951. Originally refusing to operate the aircraft after mid-January of that year, a subsequent deal reached between the airline and the pilots union extended operations of the Martin 2-0-2 until March, pending the acquisition of replacement aircraft. By April of 1951, however, reports of the dissatisfaction felt by Northwest pilots concerning this aircraft's safety record began appearing in the media.[11] One year later, on April 9, 1952, a Martin 2-0-2 owned by Northwest, but leased to Japan Air Lines, was lost in Japan with 37 lives after crashing into a mountain. Ironically, many of the aircraft leased by

Northwest during its program to replace the Martin 2-0-2 were DC-3s and DC-4s, the exact aircraft the troubled airliner had been intended to replace.[12]

From its 2-0-2 design, Martin developed its much more successful Model 4-0-4. Other than having a pressurized fuselage stretched by 3 feet 4 inches, this aircraft shared the same overall dimensions and passenger accommodation capabilities of its predecessor. The primary customers for the Martin 4-0-4 were Eastern Airlines and Trans World Airlines, which together accounted for all but two of the 103 examples built during the 4-0-4 production run.[13] Whereas the 2-0-2 was plagued with a poor safety record, the much-improved 4-0-4 earned a reputation as being both a safe and reliable aircraft throughout its operational career. The Martin 4-0-4 was the final commercial airliner produced by the Martin Company.

During the early 1960s, turbine powered aircraft began replacing the Martin 2-0-2 and 4-0-4 in scheduled commercial service. Today, the only known Martin 2-0-2 remaining in existence resides at the Aviation Hall of Fame & Museum of New Jersey.

Chapter Five
The Danger of Ice

The twin-engine bomber was making its way through the dark skies over Illinois towards the O'Hare International Airport. The day, January 15, 1951, was but a few hours old as this aircraft, a B -26C Invader assigned to the Illinois Air National Guard, prepared to land at an airfield that later became the busiest airport in the world.[1] Nearing its destination, however, the bomber encountered icing conditions, thus necessitating a diversion to an alternate airfield. Struggling to get their wounded craft to a safe landing, the crew of the propeller-driven aircraft was waging a losing battle against the unforgiving forces arrayed against them.

The B-26 was developed by the Douglas Aircraft Company during World War II as the A-26 Invader. This aircraft was the result of a requirement issued by the U.S. Army Air Corps in November 1940 calling for an aircraft that would supersede another of the Douglas Company's designs, the A-20 Havoc. The A-20 had entered production during 1939, and the new aircraft would draw heavily from its design. The specifications set forth in the USAAC requirement called for an aircraft that would be stronger and faster than the A-20 Havoc. In addition, the new design was to carry a heavier defensive armament and be capable of performing shorter takeoffs and landings than its predecessor.[2]

Although the first flight of the prototype did not take place until July of the following year, the United States Army Air Forces (USAAF) committed to full-scale production of the A-26 in October 1941.[3] Intended to not only replace the service's A-20 Havoc, but also the B-25 Mitchell, and B-26 Marauder, the A-26 Invader suffered a series of engineering and manufacturing setbacks that delayed its introduction into combat until 1944. Even then, concerns over the aircraft's functionality ran high. This is evidenced by the fact that the first four aircraft assigned to the Fifth Air Force during mid-1944 for operations in the Southwest Pacific were grounded prior to accumulating a total of 175 flight hours.[4]

Despite its faults, the USAAF remained committed to the A-26 Invader, a fact reinforced by its ordering of some 4,000 examples between mid-1944 and April 1945. The end of the war in August 1945, however, signaled the beginning of a dramatic reduction in the size of the United States military. As such, the 4,000 before mentioned units placed on order during the last months of the conflict were cancelled. Production of the A-26 Invader ended in 1945, with the last of 2,451 examples accepted by the Army Air Forces being delivered early the following year.

After operating as a semi-autonomous organization of the U.S. Army during World War II, the United States Air Force became an independent branch of the U.S. military in September of 1947. In June of the following year, the A-26 Invader was redesignated as the B-26 Invader to reflect the decision to eliminate the "A" designation denoting attack aircraft in favor of "B" for bomber. By this time, the B-26 Marauder had been phased-out of service, so there was little confusion over the designation change.

A restored B-26C Invader on display at the National Museum of the US Air Force in Dayton, Ohio. (USAF)

During the late 1940s, the Air Force continued its program of reequipping units operating the A-20 Havoc, B-25 Mitchell, and B-26 Marauder with the Invader. During this timeframe, a general demobilization of forces also prompted the transfer of a large number of these twin-engine bombers to the Air National Guard.[5]

One such example is the assignment of a B-26C Invader, serial number 44-35736, to the 126th Composite Group of the Illinois Air National Guard based at the O'Hare International Airport, seventeen miles northwest of downtown Chicago.

Incorporating a glass nose, the C model of the Douglas Invader was easily distinguishable from the more heavily produced B model which had a solid nose that housed from six to eight .50 caliber machine guns.[6] Powered by two Pratt & Whitney R-2800 radial engines, the B-26C Invader had a top speed of 373 mph, and a range of 1,400 miles. Measuring 51 feet 3 inches in length, and with a wingspan of 70 feet, this aircraft weighed 35,000 pounds when loaded. Although widely variable, the B-26C's typical armament consisted of two forward firing .50 caliber machine guns, with four other such guns located in two remotely controlled gun turrets. In addition to these weapons, this aircraft was able to carry up to 4,000 pounds of bombs in an internal bomb bay, while an additional 2,000 pounds of ordinance could be mounted under the wings.[7]

On the morning of January 15, 1951, 44-35736 was returning to O'Hare on the final segment of an overnight training flight that had taken it some 720 miles south to the Barksdale Air Force Base, Louisiana.[8] In command of the twin-engine bomber was its pilot, 1st Lieut. Myron A. Bourland. The remaining crew consisted of 1st Lieut. Frank R. Henderson, bombardier/ navigator, and Corporal Claude W. Bourland, engineer and brother of the pilot. Also aboard the B-26C on this fateful flight were two passengers, Captain David W. Schneider, an army reserve officer, and Corporal Ralph A. Moeller. All five aboard were residents of Illinois, with 1st Lieut. Henderson and Capt. Schneider residing in Highland Park and Crystal Lake respectively, while Corp. Moeller and the two Bourland brothers lived in Chicago.[9]

At 3:40 a.m., the control tower at O'Hare received a transmission from 44-35736 reporting that it was accumulating a heavy layer of ice on its wings.[10] As icing can disrupt the critical balance of airflow over the contour of the wing, thereby leading to a loss of lift and lowering the aircraft's stall speed, such atmospheric conditions are among the most dangerous a pilot

A B-26 conducting a bombing mission against a Communist target during the Korean War. (Defense Imagery)

can encounter. Realizing the enormity of the situation, controllers on the ground instructed 1st Lieut. Bourland to attempt a landing at the Glenview Naval Air Station, just northeast of O'Hare.

As it neared the airfield, however, the B-26 crashed into a field near Willow Road and just east of Lehigh Road in the city of Glenview, barely 100 yards short of the air station's boundary.[11] Occurring at approximately 4:05 a.m., the impact caused the light bomber to erupt into flames, killing all five persons aboard. Taking place so close to the airfield's perimeter, numerous personnel at the naval air station observed the crash. A number of witnesses to the crash reported that the initial blast was followed about ten seconds later by a second explosion.

Nearby, two sheriff department police officers, Peter Guttillo and Joseph Ludtke, witnessed the crash from their patrol car and rushed to the scene. Although arriving at the crash site barely two minutes later, the intense heat of the blaze prevented the two officers from approaching to within thirty feet of the flaming wreckage.[12]

When the bomber crashed, its fuselage came close to striking a farmhouse before coming to a stop. Wreckage from the doomed aircraft was strewn over a wide area, roughly equivalent to one half mile in diameter. One of the B-26's engines was located a block away from the primary crash site. Despite the widespread devastation, there were no injuries among those living in the area.

In common with most bomber aircraft built during World War II, the B-26C Invader was not equipped with any onboard deicing equipment. Despite the widespread use of deicing boots and bleed air systems in subsequent aircraft designs, icing conditions, such as those encountered in this story, remain a danger to air travelers to the present day. As such, this atmospheric phenomenon has been identified as the cause, or a contributing factor, in a number of aircraft accidents, including the crash of American Eagle Flight 4184 near Roselawn, Indiana on October 31, 1994, which killed 68 people.

The B-26 Invader went on to have a long career with the U.S. Air Force, participating heavily in both the Korean War and the conflict in Southeast Asia prior to its retirement in 1972. Besides its operations with the USAF, the Douglas Invader saw widespread service throughout the world with numerous civil and military operators. Today, several examples of this exceptional aircraft remain in existence. In addition to Invaders displayed in museums or in some state of restoration, several others remain in a flyable condition.

Chapter Six
...a "marvelous job" of crash-landing...

The atmospheric conditions at Buffalo, New York on the afternoon of January 20, 1954 could be termed as anything but excellent flying weather. Sitting at the easternmost end of Lake Erie, Buffalo owed much of its early growth during the early 1800s as being the western terminus of the Erie Canal. When passenger and airmail service began during the 1920s, the city once again capitalized upon its location on the route between cities on the eastern seaboard such as Boston and New York and other large cities to the west such as Cleveland, Detroit, and Chicago. The same location that allowed Buffalo to grow economically, however, also makes it very susceptible to rapidly changing weather conditions, especially during the winter months. On this particular day, a low pressure weather system moving east over Lake Erie brought strong winds and decreasing visibility to the second most populous city in the state of New York. At 4:18 that afternoon, an American Airlines Convair 240 landed at the Buffalo Municipal Airport.[1] A little more than twenty minutes later, this aircraft would once again be in motion as it accelerated down the runway bound for Detroit. Even as the twin-engine airliner struggled into the air, however, a hidden mechanical defect would set into motion a sequence of events that resulted in the flight coming to an end only a mile south of the airfield.

Following the end of the Second World War, American

Airlines began searching for an aircraft to replace its fleet of Douglas DC-3s. This resulted in Consolidated Vultee Aircraft Corporation (Convair) developing its 30-seat Model 110, the prototype of which first flew on July 8, 1946. By this time, however, American Airlines had opted to order the Model 240 (CV-240), a design based on the Model 110 but capable of seating forty passengers. Just eight months later, on March 16, 1947, the first Convair 240 (NX-90849) embarked upon its maiden flight at San Diego, California.[2]

Unlike its nearest competitor, the Martin 2-0-2, the Convair 240 incorporated a pressurized fuselage. This feature allowed passengers to travel in comfort while the aircraft operated at high altitudes. Powered by a pair of 2,400 horsepower Pratt & Whitney R-2800 Double Wasp radial engines, the CV-240 had a cruising speed of 213 knots (245 mph). Series production began during late 1947, and by the middle of the following year Convair had received orders for over one hundred and fifty examples of its new airliner. The largest single order, for seventy -five planes, came from the aircraft's launch customer, American Airlines. Other domestic airlines placing orders for the CV-240 included Continental, Pan American Airways, and Western.[3]

Having received its first Convair 240 earlier that year, American Airlines inaugurated scheduled service with the type on June 1, 1948. During the mid-1930s, American Airlines began using Buffalo as a major hub along its routes to and from Boston and New York City. By the early 1950s, these operations had expanded to the point that the arrival and departure of aircraft belonging to American Airlines at the Buffalo Municipal Airport was a common occurrence.

Flight Number 767 was but one of the many such flights American Airlines had scheduled to transit the Great Lakes region on Wednesday, January 20, 1954. Scheduled to originate at Boston, the route for this flight would terminate at St. Louis, Missouri. While transiting over this route, a number of intermediate stops would be made along the way, one of which was at Buffalo. Bad weather over the first segment of the route, however, prompted the rescheduling of the flight so that it originated at Albany, New York. Assigned to this flight was a Convair 240, registered as N94244, which had been delivered to American Airlines on August 13, 1948. Now designated as Flight 6767, the Convair 240 departed Albany under the command of Captain Sanderson. While taking off, the crew noticed a sluggish reading on the left brake mean effective pressure (BMEP) instrument. Proving to be a momentary fluctuation, this problem did not reoccur throughout the remainder of the flight to Buffalo.[4]

At 4:18 p.m., after struggling with headwinds and turbulence as they flew across the state, the crew of N94244 brought their silver airliner in for a safe landing at the Buffalo Municipal Airport. While at Buffalo, a new crew consisting of Captain Charles A. Hilborn, First Officer John A. Ryan, and Stewardess Patricia Dixon, would come aboard the Convair 240.

Prior to turning N94244 over to the new crew, Captain Sanderson informed both the airline's maintenance department and the incoming captain of the fluctuation noticed on the BMEP instrumentation during the takeoff at Albany. As this discrepancy was experienced only momentarily, and was considered as being a condition commonly experienced during

47

cold weather, it was not written up for any further corrective action.

The flight crew boarding N94244 at Buffalo was highly experienced in operating this type of aircraft. Captain Charles A. Hilborn, of Kenmore, New York, had been employed by American Airlines since October 15, 1942. During his flight career, the 32 year-old captain had logged 4,389 of his 8,671 total flight hours aboard Convair airliners. At 36 years in age, First Officer John A. Ryan had amassed a total of 4,249 hours of flight time, of which 2,082, or nearly half, were earned aboard the Convair 240. First Officer Ryan had been employed by American Airlines since June 18, 1951.

Shortly after its arrival at Buffalo, ground crews began preparing the airliner for its immediate departure to Detroit, the next segment of Flight 6767. Prior to boarding the aircraft, Captain Hilborn reviewed the weather conditions over his intended route to the Willow Run Airport, just southwest of Detroit. His instructions from the airline's dispatch office also

A Convair 240 operating for American Airlines. (Author's Collection)

listed the airports at Cleveland and Columbus, Ohio as alternate landing fields in the event that weather conditions prevented a safe landing at Detroit.

Aboard the airliner for this flight were twenty-one passengers, some of whom had seats that afforded a splendid view through one of the aircraft's twenty cabin windows. Shortly after the last passenger had boarded the aircraft, the crew began taxiing towards runway 23. With a takeoff weight 40,541 pounds, the Convair 240 was well below its maximum allowable gross weight of 41,200 pounds.

At 4:40 p.m., barely twenty-two minutes after its arrival at Buffalo, N94244 began accelerating down runway 23. After proceeding approximately 2,800 feet down the runway, the airliner lifted off during what so far had been a perfectly normal takeoff. Mindful of the sluggish BMEP reading experienced by the previous crew during their departure from Albany, Captain Hilborn had maintained a close watch for any discrepancies on that instrument. Throughout the preflight procedures and the subsequent takeoff, however, this gauge had indicated entirely normal readings.

Upon leaving the ground, the crew raised the landing gear as the aircraft began its ascent into the blustery skies. Moments after takeoff, however, First Officer Ryan noticed the illumination of the feathering button light for the left engine. This indicated that the auto-feathering system was in the process of feathering the left propeller. After a visual check of the left propeller through the captain's side window, the crew responded by disarming the aircraft's auto-feathering system. As part of this process, Captain Hilborn pulled the feathering button to its neutral position. This effort proved unsuccessful, and within a few seconds, the left propeller feathered and the engine suddenly lost power and stopped.

With its right engine still operating at full takeoff power, the airliner was able to maintain a positive climb at an airspeed of 122 knots (140 mph). Believing that his aircraft could not continue climbing with only one operable engine, Captain Hilborn brought its nose down to level off at approximately 250 feet above the ground. After leveling off, the captain put the aircraft into a shallow left turn even as he directed his copilot to begin attempts to restart the left engine.

To perform this procedure, First Officer Ryan placed the feathering button in the unfeather position. This commanded the rotation of blades to an angle at which the propeller would begin to windmill, thereby turning the engine. This resulted in the engine only reaching a maximum of 600 revolutions per minute (rpm), far below the 1,300 rpm required for engine restart. As the copilot continued his efforts to get the left engine running again, Captain Hilborn began feeling a buffeting sensation through his control column.

By this time, the ill-fated airliner had completed a turn of approximately 180 degrees from its original takeoff heading. Viewing the terrain ahead, Captain Hilborn had serious doubts the struggling aircraft would be able to clear a number of obstacles in its flight path, including some high tension power lines. Faced with this possibility, the 32 year-old captain decided to perform a crash landing in a field about one mile south of the airport.

Settling onto the ground on a heading of 71 degrees, the

The Convair 240 was developed specifically to meet a requirement issued by American Airlines to replace its fleet of DC-3 airliners. (Author's Collection)

Convair 240 slid across a field for an additional 1,200 feet before finally coming to a stop. While proceeding along the ground, the aircraft struck a number of trees, during which the left wing, outboard of the engine nacelle, and the left horizontal stabilizer were torn away. Meanwhile, the impact with trees along the aircraft's path also opened up a hole in the left side of the fuselage, near the cockpit. The airliner's final resting spot was only about 100 yards from the power lines that Captain Hilborn had so desperately wished to avoid. While the aircraft was destroyed in the crash landing, everyone onboard managed to survive the accident.

Of the twenty-four occupants aboard the downed airliner, only seven required medical treatment when they emerged from the mangled plane. Consisting mostly of cuts and bruises, none of these injuries was considered as being overly serious. Nonetheless, at least four persons were admitted to local hospitals. After the accident, several of the passengers praised Captain Hilborn for a "marvelous job" of crash-landing the American Airlines plane.[5]

Receiving notification of the accident within minutes of its happening, the Civil Aeronautics Board hastened to dispatch a team of investigators to Buffalo. An examination of N94244's wreckage revealed no evidence of an airframe failure prior to the crash. Both of the airliner's engines were found to have sustained only minor damage during the impact and the subsequent skid along the ground.

During a test run of the recovered left engine, investigators determined that the torquemeter boost pump was producing only 65 pounds per square inch (psi) of pressure at an engine speed of 2,200 rpm. This reading contrasted heavily with the boost pump's normal 250 psi operating pressure at a speed of 1,600 rpm. The removal and disassembly of this component revealed that its drive gear had suffered a fatigue failure. It was therefore determined that the failure of the torquemeter boost pump activated the left propeller's auto-feathering system. Following the replacement of this defective component, the left engine was restarted and found capable of operating within satisfactory parameters.

During the investigation, examiners ascertained that the slow response noticed on the BMEP gauge was most likely not indicative of an impending power plant failure. Regardless, the Board did not hesitate to criticize the apparent lack of attention placed upon this discrepancy, a fact duly noted in the final accident report.[6]

While being questioned by investigators, First Officer Ryan stated that he probably held the feathering button in the unfeather position for longer than two seconds. Furthermore, this same process was repeated several times as Ryan continued his attempts to restart the left engine. Believing that holding the button in the unfeather position would expedite the unfeathering of the propeller blades, the 36 year-old first officer did not realize that such an action would actually result in the blades moving back and forth in a six-degree of travel in the high pitch range, a condition termed as "hunting." The turbulence created by the rapid pitch angle changes in the windmilling left propeller also induced the buffeting sensation Captain Hilborn felt emanating from his control column.

A review of the flight manual provided by American Airlines to the pilots of its fleet of Convair 240s revealed a discrepancy that directly contributed to the crash of Flight 6767. In this handbook, the unfeathering procedure required to achieve the 1,300 rpm engine starting speed included the following statement:

> "For unfeathering[,] the button must be pulled out and held out as required to accomplish unfeathering…"

In this statement, the word "held" was underlined to emphasize its implied importance. Emergency procedures appearing elsewhere in the flight manual, however, warned against holding the feathering button in the unfeathering position for more than two seconds. Investigators concluded that if the correct unfeathering procedure had been followed, the left engine could have been restarted. Dependent upon at what point in the short flight an engine restart had been accomplished, it may have been possible for the crew to avoid the crash landing. Following this accident, American Airlines corrected its flight manuals to prevent any further incidents of this nature.[7]

When the Civil Aeronautics Board issued its final report concerning the crash of N94244 on May 24, 1954, it identified two factors that contributed heavily to the accident. The following is an excerpt from that report:

> The Board determines that the probable cause of this accident was (1) a mechanical failure of the torquemeter boost pump that automatically feathered the left propeller immediately after becoming airborne, and (2) the use of an incorrect procedure for unfeathering which resulted from the ambiguity of the instructions for unfeathering contained in the company's manual.

Following the completion of 571 examples, production of the Convair 240 ended in 1958. As the production list included 365 T -29 aircrew trainer aircraft and 26 C-131A Samaritans for the U.S. Air Force, sales of this aircraft was by no means limited to civilian operators.[8] The aircraft also went on to serve for many years with the U.S. Navy and Coast Guard.

The design of the Convair 240 was used as the basis for a slightly larger model, the CV-340, which first flew in October 1951. Equipped with more efficient engines than its predecessor, this airliner was capable of carrying up to 44 passengers. Embarking on its maiden flight in 1955, the subsequent Convair 440 (CV-440) retained the same basic dimensions of the CV-340 while featuring additional operational and passenger comfort refinements. As turboprop technology matured, a number of Convair 240, 340, and 440s were repowered with this type of engine, thus extending the operational lives of these aircraft. Beginning in 1965, thirty-nine Convair 240s were repowered with Rolls Royce Dart turboprop engines. Following conversion, these aircraft were assigned the Convair 600 (CV-600) designation.[9] Many Convair 600s enjoyed lengthy careers, the last such example being retired in 2012.

Chapter Seven
"...a descent at too high an airspeed..."

During the latter part of the Second World War, the United Kingdom established the Brabazon Committee to explore the needs of the postwar civil aircraft market. One of the requirements identified by this commission was for the production of a short-haul airliner for European routes. Specified in its final report as the Brabazon Type II, this requirement called for the development of both a piston-powered design (Type IIA), and an aircraft equipped with turboprop engines (Type IIB).

A turboprop engine consists of a gas turbine which drives a propeller through a gearbox. The majority of the turbine's thrust output in this type of powerplant is converted into shaft power, therefore its exhaust gasses provide only a minimal contribution in propelling the aircraft. The use of turboprop engines is popular in small to medium size commercial and military aircraft.

The recommendations of the Brabazon Committee resulted in the development of Vickers-Armstrongs VC2 design. On March 9, 1946, the UK's Ministry of Supply ordered two prototypes of this proposal, which following a series of changes had been redesignated as the Vickers Type 609 and given the name Viceroy. A subsequent switch in engines from the Armstrong Siddeley Mamba to the Rolls Royce Dart prompted the design being redesignated as the V.630. Although the Dart engine was considered as being somewhat primitive compared to the Mamba, the aircraft's chief designer, George Edwards, felt that the Rolls Royce turboprop possessed a greater level of reliability. A year after the two prototypes were ordered, international politics influenced the changing of the aircraft's name from Viceroy to Viscount following India gaining its independence from Britain.[1]

Registered as G-AHRF, the first prototype flew on July 16, 1948. Just two months later, however, Vickers was dealt a serious blow when its primary customer for the Viscount, British European Airways (BEA), opted to purchase twenty Airspeed Ambassadors instead. In spite of this, testing of the first prototype continued, with a restricted certificate of airworthiness being issued on August 19, 1949. Concurrently, the second prototype was redirected for use as a Ministry research aircraft, while plans for a third prototype were abandoned.

As the 32-passenger capacity of the V.630 could be considered too small by its potential customers, Vickers began development of a stretched version during 1948, which it designated as the V.700. Lengthening the fuselage by 88 inches allowed this variant to carry 47 passengers. Another change included extending each wing root by 30 inches, thereby providing an increased wingspan for added lift while at the same time reducing noise in the cabin by moving the inboard engines further from the fuselage.

Even as the V.700 prototype was undergoing its final assembly, the first prototype (V.630) received permission on July 27, 1950 to conduct one month of scheduled airline operations. When G-

AHRF departed London on its first of thirty-six trips to Paris, it not only became the first turboprop airliner to enter commercial service, but also the first powered by any type of turbine engine.[2]

The first V.700 prototype, registered as G-AMAV, embarked upon its maiden flight on August 28, 1950. By this time, Vickers had already received an order from British European Airways for twenty examples of the Viscount, under the V.701 designation. The first of these production aircraft flew on August 20, 1952, with deliveries to the airline beginning early the following year.

During 1952, representatives from Trans-Canada Air Lines (TCA) arrived at Vickers to begin discussions concerning the purchase of the Viscount. Though the number of engineering changes requested by the airline grew quickly, Vickers, desperate to break into the North American market, made every effort to accommodate TCA's requests. The negotiations proved successful when Trans-Canada Air Lines ordered 15 Viscounts in November 1952.

On April 1, 1955, the Viscount entered revenue service for TCA on the Montreal to Winnipeg route. By November of that year, service with the type had expanded to include fourteen cities. The Viscount proved to be a popular aircraft with the traveling public, enabling it to enjoy load factors exceeding 80 percent during its first nine months of operation.[3]

Among the aircraft delivered to TCA against its initial contract (the airline eventually acquired 51 Viscounts) was an example registered as CF-TGR. Powered by four Rolls Royce Dart 506 engines, this aircraft was accepted by Trans-Canada Air Lines on June 23, 1955, after which it was placed on the air carrier's

Trans-Canada Air Lines (TCA) was the first airline in North America to purchase the Vickers Viscount. (Author's Collection)

network of routes stretching across Canada and into the United States.

A little over one year later, on July 9, 1956, CF-TGR arrived at Chicago, Illinois as Trans-Canada Air Lines Flight 303. Originating at Montreal, Quebec, the westward flight to the windy city had been uneventful with the exception of a radio problem that was corrected during a stopover at Toronto.

Following refueling and the boarding of thirty-one passengers, the crew of the Viscount prepared for the departure from Chicago. As it made its way back to Montreal, the turboprop airliner, now operating as Flight 304, would retrace its previous route in the opposite direction. Prior to arriving at the largest city in the province of Quebec, the Viscount was scheduled to make two intermediate stops, one at Toronto, the other at Ottawa.

Commanding Flight 304 was Captain R. D. Smuck, whom was performing a route competency check of Captain A. C. Adamson. Since being employed by TCA, Captain Smuck, age 40, had amassed 9,714 flight hours, 317 of which were earned aboard the Vickers Viscount. Although Captain Adamson, at age 34, was the younger of the two pilots aboard the airliner as it departed the gate at Chicago, he actually had more flight hours with the airline than his evaluator. Since being employed by Trans-Canada Air Lines, Adamson had accumulated just under 9,976 total flight hours, of which 218 were in the Viscount.

With its four Dart turboprops producing their distinctive whine, CF-TGR departed Chicago four minutes after one o'clock in the afternoon.[4] With a gross weight of 54,179 pounds, the aircraft was some 3,221 pounds below its maximum allowable takeoff weight. In accordance with the instrument flight rules (IFR) flight plan filed prior to takeoff, the Viscount climbed to a cruising altitude of 19,000 feet.

The flight proceeded along normally as the turboprop airliner made its way across Lake Michigan and then over the state that shares the same name with that body of water. At around 1:45 p.m., however, the routine nature of the flight came to an abrupt end when the crew noticed a temporary drop in the revolutions per minute (rpm) of the No. 4 engine. During this event, the engine's speed dropped by some 200 to 300 revolutions below its normal 13,600 rpm at cruising speed. A few moments later, the engine readings returned to normal.

About five minutes later, as the aircraft neared Flat Rock, Michigan, the speed of the No. 4 engine increased rapidly to approximately 14,000 rpm. In such instances of an overspeed, it is prudent to feather the propeller attached to the affected engine. Feathering a variable pitch propeller, such as those fitted to the Viscount, involves orienting the pitch of each blade parallel to the airflow in order to reduce drag. This allows a multi-engine aircraft to maintain altitude on its remaining engines. A few moments after engine No. 4 began to overspeed, the crew attempted to feather its propeller using both automatic and manual systems. Neither of these produced results, and the engine's overspeed continued to increase.

As efforts to feather the malfunctioning engine continued, the airspeed of the airliner began to drop. This resulted in a corresponding decrease in the noise emanating from the malfunctioning engine. To compensate for the loss of airspeed, the crew increased power on the three good engines. While this action regained some of the lost airspeed, it had the effect of increasing both the sound and rpm of the No. 4 engine.

Faced with these difficulties, the crew of the Viscount contacted the Traffic Control Center at Detroit at 1:51 p.m. to declare an emergency. After receiving permission to perform an emergency descent to a lower altitude, the pilots reduced power on the three responsive engines. In their rush to get their aircraft on the ground within the shortest possible time, the crew flew the descent at nearly the maximum possible speed, a course of action that would have catastrophic consequences.

Just two minutes after declaring an emergency, the Viscount was nearing 9,000 feet when the propeller on the No. 4 engine separated from the aircraft. Following the catastrophic failure, one of the propeller blades struck the No. 3 engine. Passing completely through that engine's oil cooler, a piece of this blade penetrated the fuselage. Entering the passenger cabin near the two most forward rows of seats, the fragment of the propeller blade struck and killed one passenger. The blade, along with debris from the fuselage puncture, also injured four other passengers. As the cabin had been depressurized by this time, there was no explosive decompression when the fuselage was pierced.

Oblivious of what had just taken place in the cabin, the pilots continued their descent towards 3,000 feet. Although the cruise portion of the flight had been conducted above a cloud layer, the crew was able to maintain a visual reference to the ground throughout the descent by finding breaks in the clouds. As the Viscount reached 3,000 feet, the crew reapplied power to the three operable engines. As power ramped up, it became obvious that there was now a problem with the No. 3 engine. Gauges in the cockpit indicated that this engine would produce no more than 11,500 rpm, and within a few moments, the fire warning activated. This prompted the pilots to conduct an engine fire procedure, which included feathering the propeller on the affected engine.

Flying with only the two portside engines operating, the pilots continued their descent towards Windsor, Ontario, some 20 miles to the northeast. About ten minutes following the in-flight disintegration of the No. 4 propeller, CF-TGR landed safely at the Windsor Airport. It was only after they had brought the wounded Viscount in for a landing that Captains Smuck and Adamson became aware of the fatality and injuries suffered by those in the cabin.

When the tip of the propeller blade entered the fuselage, it struck Mrs. Robert Lippert of Rochester, Minnesota, killing her instantly. Seated with Mrs. Lippert were her two sons, Robert, 3, and James, 21 months. While both of the boys escaped serious injury by the narrowest of margins, Robert later required medical care for shock.

Other passengers taken to the hospital included Christopher Dumbell, of Dubuque, Iowa, along with his wife, Donna, and son, Donald, all of whom had suffered leg injuries. Meanwhile Donovan Stevens of Mundelein, Illinois required medical treatment for severe cuts to his neck. Another casualty was Rita Tobin, one of the two stewardesses aboard the plane, who received treatment for shock.[5]

With the actual accident occurring over the United States aboard a Canadian registered airliner, which had in fact continued on to land in Canada, the investigation required a mutual effort by both countries. As such, the Civil Aeronautics Board (CAB) and Canada's Department of Transport established a joint board of inquiry to investigate the incident under the requirements of both nations.[6]

An inspection of the No. 4 engine revealed that the driven bevel gear of the bevel box drive had sustained a fatigue failure, resulting in the rotation of the drive becoming completely disrupted. In this particular type of engine, the fuel pump, oil pump, and propeller control unit are all driven by the bevel box drive. Investigators were able to analyze engine No. 4's rpm indicating and propeller feathering systems up to the point at which the front part of the powerplant had separated from the aircraft. This examination revealed that both systems were capable of functioning properly, a conclusion confirmed by subsequent testing of the individual components at a facility in Winnipeg, Manitoba.[7]

After analyzing the available data, investigators were unable to conclude if the temporary drop of rpm in the No. 4 engine had any relevance to subsequent events. It was established, however, that the initial overspeed of the engine to approximately 14,000 rpm occurred concurrently with the failure of the driven bevel gear, which failed to the extent that rotation of the bevel box drive was stopped completely. It was further determined that at this stage of the mechanical difficulties, the No. 4 propeller could have been successfully feathered.

With its blades set at a fine pitch angle for flight, the propeller continued to rotate the engine, which by this time had lost lubrication pressure. The failure of the high-speed pinion led to the propeller oil transfer housing being damaged, which created a loss in pressure to deflect the propeller blade angle. Therefore, when the crew made their initial attempt at feathering the propeller, it was already impossible to do so.[8]

During the rapid descent from 19,000 feet, the No. 4 propeller continued to spin at an increasing rate until it finally failed at approximately 9,000 feet. With the exception of the tip of the No. 2 blade, which entered the passenger cabin, all four of the blades, along with the propeller's hub and shaft, were located separately, but within the same general area, near Flat Rock. Other than impact damage, none of this debris exhibited any irregularities such as a manufacturing defect. Subsequent information provided by the propeller's manufacturer, Rotol Limited, confirmed that the stresses experienced by Flight 304's No. 4 propeller exceeded the design limits of its blade retention strength.

While conceding that an uncontrolled propeller was a contingency for which the Viscount training program did not address, the CAB was nonetheless critical of the crew's actions leading up to the accident. In its report, the Board pointed out that the pilots should have recognized that the sound of engine No. 4's overspeed increased and decreased in relation to the increase and decrease of the aircraft's airspeed. Recognizing this, a slower airspeed should have been flown to reduce the stress placed upon the unfeathered propeller. It was therefore concluded that rather than ordering a rapid descent, Captain Smuck should have maintained a moderate airspeed, which would have prevented the failure of the No. 4 propeller.

On March 11, 1957, the CAB published the results of its investigation into the propeller failure of Trans-Canada Flight 304. The following was determined by the Board as being the probable cause of the incident:

> The Board determines that the probable cause of this accident was the inflight separation of the No. 4 propeller as a result of excessive loads induced by a descent at too high an airspeed while the propeller was windmilling decoupled from the engine and its r.p.m was known to be uncontrolled.

Following the accident, Trans-Canada Air Lines continued to be a loyal user of the Vickers Viscount. While several of these turboprop airliners were still in service when the airline became Air Canada on January 1, 1965, CF-TGR was not among them.[9] In early 1963, this aircraft was withdrawn from service, and remained in storage for two years before being sold to William C. Wold Associates, an aircraft broker. Following this transaction,

Beginning in 1956, Capital Airlines began acquiring a large fleet of Vickers Viscounts. When this carrier was absorbed by United Airlines in 1961, these aircraft were repainted with their new owner's livery before being retired in 1969. (Author's Collection)

the Viscount was registered in the United States as N911H. In June 1965, this aircraft was sold to Air Inter, a domestic French airline, and placed into service as F-BNAX. The aging Viscount continued in operation for Air Inter until being withdrawn and scrapped during 1975.

The last of the 444 Vickers Viscounts produced left the factory during 1964. Of this total, 438 were delivered to various customers around the world, including CAAC (Civil Aviation Administration of China). In fact, when CAAC took delivery of the last six Viscounts built, these aircraft became the first Western built airliners acquired by the Chinese airline.[10]

Chapter Eight
"Pull it up!"

During the early morning hours of August 28, 1958, a DC-6B belonging to Northwest Airlines taxied onto the runway at the Wold-Chamberlain Field just outside of Minneapolis, Minnesota. Though the night sky was clear, there were patches of dense ground fog in the area. With a crew of four and fifty-eight passengers aboard, the four-engine airliner began its takeoff roll. As the aircraft gathered speed on its journey down the runway, there was nothing out of the ordinary to warn those aboard that their lives were now in jeopardy.

Built by the Douglas Aircraft Company, the DC-6 originated from a 1944 requirement issued by the U.S. Army Air Forces (USAAF) for an upgraded variant of the C-54 Skymaster, the military version of the DC-4. This resulted in the XC-112 design, which was essentially a DC-4 with uprated Pratt & Whitney R-2800 Double Wasp engines. This proposal was short lived, however, as it was dropped in preference to a scaled up version of the aircraft designated as the XC-112A. This design combined the R-2800 engines from the original proposal with a longer fuselage and cabin pressurization. The latter feature permitted flights to be conducted at higher altitudes, thus providing improved cruising speeds and better fuel economy.

With Douglas test pilot John Martin in command, the only XC-112A built flew for the first time on February 15, 1946. Following four months of initial testing, the USAAF accepted delivery of this aircraft on June 2 of that year, after which it received the YC-112A designation.[1]

Even as the XC-112A was conducting its early testing, Douglas was putting the finishing touches on the first true civil prototype of the DC-6. Registered as NX90701 (later N90701), this aircraft embarked upon its maiden flight on June 29, 1946. After completing its test program, this aircraft was delivered to American Airlines in April of the following year. Meanwhile, delivery of the first production aircraft to the type's two launch customers, American and United Airlines, took place on March 28, 1947.[2]

With a wingspan of 117 feet 6 inches and a length of 100 feet 7 inches, the DC-6 was capable of accommodating a maximum of 85 passengers in a high-density layout. Powered by four R-2800 Double Wasp radial engines, the airliner had a maximum cruising speed of 274 knots (315 mph) at an altitude of 20,000 feet. At that height, thanks to its automatic pressurization system, the aircraft's occupants were able to enjoy a cabin altitude equivalent to 8,000 feet.

During early 1948, Douglas began developing a freighter variant that was designated as the DC-6A. While retaining the same wingspan, this model had a fuselage 5 feet longer than that of the standard DC-6. Flying for the first time on September 29, 1949, the DC-6A, with its strengthened structure, was able to carry a 29,500 pound payload.[3]

Building upon the DC-6A, Douglas developed a passenger only variant designated as the DC-6B. Initially marketed to the airlines in 1950, the first DC-6B took to the skies on February 2, 1951. While this aircraft retained the longer fuselage of the DC-

6A, the cargo doors and reinforced cabin floor were deleted. Although the aircraft's accommodation was influenced by its operational role, the DC-6B could carry up to a maximum of 102 passengers. When production ended in November 1958, some 288 examples of the B model had been manufactured, thus making it the most popular DC-6 variant.

Following its completion at the Douglas factory on March 2, 1957, one of these aircraft was delivered to Northwest Airlines. Registered as N575, this airliner was one of twelve DC-6Bs delivered to the air carrier by the manufacturer.[4]

On August 27, 1958, N575 was operating as Flight 537 when it departed Washington D. C. on a regularly scheduled route that would terminate at Seattle, Washington. As it made its way westwards, intermediate stops would be made at Pittsburg, Cleveland, Detroit, Milwaukee, and finally Minneapolis before beginning the longest segment of the flight to Portland, Oregon.

After an uneventful flight, N575 arrived at Minneapolis, where a scheduled crew change took place. Shortly after 2:00 a.m. on the morning of August 28, 1958, the relief crew began arriving at the Wold-Chamberlain Field in preparation for the overnight flight across the western United States.[5]

The flight crew consisted of Captain James Wilkinson, whom at age 37 had completed 12,376 flight hours, of which 572 were in the DC-6. Employed by Northwest Orient since February 10, 1943, Wilkinson was well acquainted with the Douglas family of airliners. Besides being licensed to command the DC-6, he was also rated to operate the DC-3, DC-4, and DC-7.[6]

Joining Captain Wilkinson in the cockpit was First Officer Verner J. McGinness and Flight Engineer Robert R. Mielke.

69

Working for Northwest Orient Airlines since being hired on July 30, 1952, McGinness had attained 148 of his 9,089 total flight hours aboard the DC-6. Originally joining the airline as an aircraft mechanic in October of 1950, Robert Mielke had received a promotion to flight engineer on May 29, 1958.

As preparations to depart Minneapolis continued, the aircraft's only stewardess, Margaret C. Gallagher, assisted the fifty-eight passengers to their seats in the cabin. Among the group of passengers boarding the four-engine plane during the early hours of that summer morning were eleven U.S. Army troops, most of whom were en route to Fort Lewis, Washington, and two infants.

The weather forecast provided to the crew of Flight 537, specified good weather for their journey to Portland. Although the skies above Wold-Chamberlain Field were clear, there was, however, patches of ground fog that reduced visibility to a

An interior view of a Northwest Airlines DC-6B's passenger cabin. (Author's Collection)

prevailing three miles at low altitude. Additionally, transmissometer readings taken from the approach end of runway 29L indicated that drifting patches of dense fog were also present around the airfield, further restricting visibility in certain areas.[7]

Finding no discrepancies with their aircraft, the flight crew began startup procedures for the DC-6B's four Pratt & Whitney R -2800 engines. Shortly afterwards, the tower cleared N575 to taxi to runway 22. Nearing the runway, the aircraft halted in the run-up position so Flight Engineer Mielke could monitor engine performance as the throttles were advanced momentarily. With the engines operating normally, and having completed their preflight checklists, the crew of the airliner turned onto runway 22 at 3:28 a.m., and prepared to depart into the dark skies.

After Captain Wilkinson advanced the throttles to takeoff power, N575 began to move, slowly at first, but gradually accelerating as the airliner proceeded down the runway. When the DC-6B reached a speed of 105 knots (121 mph), First Officer McGinness called out "V_1," signifying that the aircraft had reached a speed after which it could no longer be safely stopped on the remaining length of the runway. Having passed the V_1 speed, Wilkinson was now committed to the takeoff, even in the event of an engine failure. A few moments later, with the DC-6B still accelerating normally, Captain Wilkinson pulled back on the control column just before the first officer reported reaching 115 knots (132 mph), the V_2 (takeoff) speed.

After becoming airborne and establishing a positive climb, Wilkinson instructed the first officer to raise the landing gear. As the DC-6B continued to gather speed, McGinness continued carrying out his responsibility of informing the captain of the increasing airspeed readings. When the airliner reached a speed of 135 knots (155 mph), Wilkinson instructed the copilot to raise the flaps.

Upon reaching an airspeed of 155 knots (178 mph), and with the DC-6B continuing to perform normally, Captain Wilkinson ordered a reduction in engine power. At this same moment, the captain's vision out the cockpit windows became obscured by the landing lights reflecting off a layer of heavy fog. Believing the airliner was still maintaining a positive rate of climb, Wilkinson turned off the landing lights. Almost simultaneously, First Officer McGinness saw a fence ahead of the aircraft and shouted "pull it up!"

Within a few moments of the first officer's warning, the Northwest airliner struck a chain link fence at the airport's southern boundary. Remaining airborne for another sixty feet, the DC-6B struck the ground some 2,900 feet from the threshold lights located at the southwest end of runway 22. Impacting the ground in a slightly nose up attitude, the ill-fated airliner skidded for another 1,600 feet before coming to rest just 30 feet short of a farmhouse owned by Jerry Christian. During its slide through the cornfield, the aircraft demolished a granary, storage shed, and a garage. The latter structure contained a new automobile, in which Mr. Christian had planned to leave a few hours later on a fishing trip.[8]

Coming to a stop on its left side, none of the exits on that side of the fuselage were usable to those aboard the shattered airliner as they struggled to find an avenue of escape. Fortunately, however, the crash had ripped a hole in the top left side of the forward fuselage. It was through this opening, that most of the passengers found their way out of the plane's mangled interior. The remaining occupants of the downed DC-6B were able to escape through a door on the right side of the aircraft and the copilot's sliding window in the cockpit.[9]

In spite of the rush to escape the burning wreckage, the evacuation of the downed DC-6B was orderly enough to allow some passengers to retrieve their luggage prior to reaching safety. While there were no fatalities in the accident, a large number of people, including all four members of the flight crew, sustained injuries which required medical treatment. The majority of those injured were taken to the Northwestern Hospital in Minneapolis, with the balance receiving treatment at the nearby Veteran's Hospital, and the Ancker Hospital in St. Paul.[10]

Describing the experiences of one of the plane's passengers, the following excerpt is from a wire story that appeared in the August 28, 1958 edition of Mitchell, South Dakota's *The Daily Republic*:

> Mrs. Wesley Gillies, 52, L[i]vonia, Mich., was sitting near an emergency door when "it happened so fast I didn't know what was going on."
> She jumped through an opening "and the co-pilot caught me." Mrs. Gillies said she thought the plane was still in the air when it actually was tumbling along the ground.

Notified within thirty minutes of the accident, the Civil Aeronautics Board (CAB) initiated an investigation into the crash of Flight 537. Arriving at the accident scene, investigators discovered that a post-crash fire, which broke out a few minutes

The C-118 Liftmaster was the militarized variant of the DC-6A. (USAF)

after the evacuation of the passengers, had consumed approximately 85 percent of the aircraft's wreckage. Nonetheless, the investigation revealed that all four of the DC-6B's engines were operating within normal parameters and generating sufficient power in the moments leading up to the crash. Additionally, there was no evidence to indicate that any form of mechanical or structural failure had contributed to the accident.

With these possible causes ruled out, the investigation focused on the actions of the crew prior to the crash. Interviews with the flight crew indicated that both pilots believed the airliner was climbing normally after taking off, despite the fact that it was actually descending. After considering the visual conditions present at the airfield on the morning of the accident, investigators theorized that the flight crew had fallen victim to a phenomenon known as pilot sensory illusion. Under such circumstances, a pilot can experience a nose-up tilt sensation, thus causing a natural tendency to push the nose of the aircraft down. The resulting acceleration can bolster this illusion, causing a sensation of a steady climb, while the aircraft is actually in a descent.

While such a phenomenon provided a reasonable explanation as to the cause of the accident, it did not account for the crew's failure in detecting the descent on their instruments. In its report, the CAB was critical of Captain Wilkinson for not utilizing all of the aircraft's instrumentation while taking off in the weather conditions existing at the time of the accident. The Board also pointed out that the rapid acceleration of the airliner shortly after takeoff should have alerted the pilots that something was wrong. During normal operating procedures, a DC-6B requires approximately 85 seconds to reach an airspeed of 155 knots (178 mph), during which time the aircraft would travel an horizontal distance equal to 15,000 feet. In the case of Flight 537, it was determined that after accelerating to 155 knots (178 mph), N575 first hit the ground in just over half that distance (7,600 feet). During his testimony, the captain of the Northwest Orient airliner stated his belief that the aircraft was still over the runway at the time it reached that speed. This reinforced the Board's view that the highly experienced captain should have realized the airliner's acceleration shortly after takeoff was far in excess of normal parameters.[11]

On July 2, 1959, nearly one year after the accident, the Civil Aeronautics Board released the findings of their investigation into the crash of Flight 537. As stated before, the report was critical of the pilot's inability to avoid the accident. To illustrate this point, the CAB report included the following statement concerning the cause of the crash:

> The Board determines that the probable cause of this accident was the pilot's inattention to flight instruments during takeoff in conditions of reduced visibility.

Following the accident, Northwest Orient Airlines updated the takeoff procedures for their fleet of DC-6B aircraft. These changes included not raising the flaps until reaching an altitude of 200 feet and a speed of 125 knots (144 mph), along with takeoff power not being reduced until the aircraft reaches a speed of at least 140 knots (161 mph). Furthermore, the new rules required the copilot to read out altimeter readings up to 500 feet in 100-foot intervals.[12]

On February 10, 1959, Douglas delivered the last DC-6 built to the Brazilian airline Lóide Aéreo Nacional.[13] With all its variants

Of the 288 DC-6Bs built, only 12 were delivered to Northwest Airlines. As a consequence, photographs of these planes are somewhat rare. This example, operated by Northeast Airlines, is virtually identical to the aircraft involved in this chapter's accident. (Author's Collection)

considered as a whole, Douglas manufactured 704 examples of the DC-6 during its production run. Following the DC-6, Douglas introduced the DC-7, which represented yet another stretch of the DC-6/6A/6B series.[14]

Although among the most advanced piston-powered passenger aircraft ever produced, the DC-6/7 series entered service at the dawn of the jet age. As a consequence, these aircraft were the last such designs developed by the Douglas Aircraft Company before its focus shifted towards the manufacture of that firm's next generation of airliners, the jet powered DC-8 and DC-9.

Today, only a small number of DC-6s remain in active service around the globe. Although their numbers continue to dwindle, a handful of these dependable aircraft continue to operate as cargo freighters into remote areas of Alaska.

Chapter Nine
A Tale of Two British Bombers

The end of the Second World War marked the beginning of the nuclear age, which in turn led to an era of worldwide tension known simply as the Cold War. As the gulf between the West, and its former wartime ally, the Soviet Union, widened, both sides embarked upon massive military programs in an attempt to deter aggression from their respective adversaries.

While the United States had emerged from the war possessing a nuclear monopoly, other nations placed a high priority upon their own programs to acquire such weapons. Aided by a highly effective espionage effort, the Soviet Union managed to detonate its first atomic bomb on August 29, 1949, just four years following the first such test conducted by the United States. Besides these two nations, the United Kingdom also pursued its own nuclear weapon program during this timeframe, and in 1952, it became the world's third nation to detonate an atomic bomb.

The development of a new British bomber to deliver an atomic weapon was initiated in 1947. Powered by turbojets, the new aircraft was intended to have twice the performance characteristics of the piston-powered bombers then in service with the Royal Air Force (RAF). In January of 1948, a contract was placed with A. V. Roe and Company (Avro) for two prototypes of its Type 698 design.[1]

Four years later, on August 30, 1952, the first prototype (XV770) took to the skies, thus making the type's maiden flight. Appearing much like a massive manta ray, thanks to its tailless delta-wing configuration, this bomber became one of the most recognizable aircraft of the Cold War era. It would be just over one year before the second prototype (VX777), with uprated Olympus 100 engines, flew for the first time in September 1953.

Designated as the Vulcan, this aircraft was one of three bomber types that entered service with RAF during the 1950s. Collectively known as the "V-Bomber" force, these aircraft represented the primary component of Britain's nuclear deterrent capability during this time. Besides the Vulcan, this group also included the Vickers Valiant and Handley Page Victor.

By mid-1956, the first of forty-five production Vulcan B.Mk.1 bombers began arriving in active-duty RAF squadrons.[2] The B.Mk.1 had a cruising speed of 607 mph (Mach 0.92) at 50,000 feet, and was capable of carrying up to 21,000 pounds of conventional or nuclear free-fall ordinance over a combat radius of some 1,700 miles.[3] This enabled the Vulcan to reach targets throughout all of Eastern Europe and large portions of the Soviet Union from its bases within the United Kingdom.

While the Vulcan was primarily committed to operations in Europe, the type deployed regularly to North America to participate in military exercises and the occasional air show. It would be during such deployments that two of these British bombers, far from home, came to grief in the Great Lakes region some two hundred miles and twenty years apart.

On October 23, 1958, the crew of a Vulcan bomber based at the

The unique planform of the Vulcan bomber, along with its engine placement, is readily apparent in this photograph. (Defense Imagery)

Royal Air Force's Waddington airbase could be found busily preparing their aircraft for a transatlantic deployment to the Lincoln Air Force Base in Nebraska.[4] Belonging to the RAF's Bomber Command's No. 83 Squadron, serial number XA908 had been delivered to the Royal Air Force the previous September, and was one of the early B.Mk.1 models of the Vulcan that began entering service during 1956.

Commanding the four-engine British bomber as it departed its base in the eastern United Kingdom was 34 year-old Flight Lt. John Willoughby Moore. Seated alongside him was the bomber's copilot, Flight Lt. Brian Peacock. The remainder of the crew aboard included Squadron Ldr. Harvey J. Scull, navigator; Flying Officer Anthony D. Baker, air electronics officer; Flight Lt. James D. Watson, navigator; and Chief Technician Edward C.

Evison, crew chief. During normal operations, the Vulcan only carried a crew of five. For this exercise, however, Evison had joined the Vulcan's regular complement to support the overseas deployment.

RAF Waddington is located just south of the city of Lincoln, Lincolnshire, and on this trip a message of friendship was being carried aboard the aircraft from the mayor of that community addressed to his counterpart at Lincoln, Nebraska.[5]

Unable to fly directly to Lincoln AFB from its base in the UK, the Vulcan was scheduled to make a stopover at Goose Bay, Labrador for crew rest and refueling. Following an uneventful 2,500 mile flight, the delta-wing bomber arrived safely at Goose Bay, where it, and its crew, spent the night. The following morning, October 24, the four engines of XA908 came to life when the aircraft thundered once again into its element by rising into the skies above the northeastern Canadian wilderness to begin the roughly 1,800 mile trek to Nebraska.

For the next few hours, Flight Lieutenant John Willoughby Moore, and his crew, guided their 180,000-pound craft across the provinces of Quebec and Ontario as they proceeded upon what thus far had been a routine flight. If all went well, the British bomber was expected to arrive at the Strategic Air Command's Lincoln AFB at approximately 4:23 (local) that afternoon. At 3:18 p.m., Detroit time, a ground station located at Erie, Pennsylvania received a report from the Vulcan bomber reporting it was at an altitude of 47,000 feet and would be passing over Flint, Michigan in thirty minutes.

Just a few minutes later, however, a radio operator at Cleveland's Municipal Airport received a frantic "Mayday!" call from XA908. In a subsequent transmission, the pilot reported that he was currently at 35,000 feet over Dresden, Ontario, a community about fifty miles northeast of Detroit, and was descending following his aircraft having suffered an electrical failure.

A subsequent transmission from the stricken bomber received a few moments later requested instructions for an emergency descent to Kellogg Field at Battle Creek, Michigan. Before ground controllers could provide this information, however, a further message transmitted from the plunging bomber pleaded for directions to any airport. This transmission was the final message received from the doomed jet.[6]

Traveling westwards, the Vulcan continued its downward descent over Lake St. Clair, finally emerging from the overcast just above the confluence of that body of water and the Detroit River. Plunging at an angle in excess of 60 degrees, the massive aircraft impacted the ground at 3:43 p.m. at a location just inside the northern city limits of Detroit, a few blocks from Grosse Pointe.

Consisting mainly of one and two story homes, the area where the accident occurred was heavily populated. The resulting explosion from the crash destroyed three houses, while reports from the accident scene indicated that at least two other residences were damaged beyond repair. The tremendous blast threw debris over a wide area, causing damage to at least fifteen other homes and businesses in the surrounding area.[7] Hot wreckage also rained down upon a local playground and hospital.

Despite the level of devastation, the six crewmembers aboard the ill-fated jet were the only fatalities caused by the crash. Newspaper accounts of the accident relate the details of a number of minor injuries being suffered by those on the ground, but none that proved to be life threatening.

During its development, designers at Avro outfitted the Vulcan with ejection seats for the pilot and copilot only. Therefore, during an accident, the only avenue of escape for the remaining crewmembers was to manually parachute out a hatch built into the floor of the crew compartment. A dubious proposition at best, this escape method is considered as having been virtually impossible to perform during this particular crash.

While initial reports from the scene ruled out the possibility that any member of the Vulcan's crew had managed to escape the aircraft during its final plunge, the discovery of the copilot's ejection seat in nearby Lake St. Clair provided some faint hope to the contrary. After an extensive search, however, recovery forces could find no trace of Flt. Lt. Brian Peacock in the cold waters of the freshwater lake.

Immediately following the crash, the government of the United Kingdom established a board of inquiry to begin an investigation into the crash of their jet bomber. This process included dispatching a team of four investigators to the United States. This group included Wing Commander Fred Miller, Wing Commander Frank Dodd, Group Captain Douglas Haig from the RAF, and Arthur E. Broomfield of the Ministry of Transport. This investigative team arrived in Detroit on October 26, and arrived at the crash site accompanied by United States Air Force officials from nearby Selfridge Air Force Base.[8]

Investigators later established that an electrical short circuit in the Vulcan's main buss bar blocked power from the generators in reaching the aircraft's systems, thereby causing a complete electrical failure. In such an event, the aircraft was equipped with an emergency battery system that should have provided up to 20 minutes of power. After just a few minutes, however, battery power failed and all power to control the aircraft was lost, thereby dooming the jet and its crew. This finding led to a modification of the Vulcan's main buss bar to prevent a similar accident.

A funeral service for the six British airmen killed in the accident was held on November 12, 1958 at the Oak Ridge Cemetery near Flat Rock, Michigan. Although the body of Flt. Lt. Brian Peacock had not yet been located, six coffins were laid to rest during this ceremony, these being carried by representatives from the Selfridge AFB. The burials reflected a long-held British tradition of burying their servicemen close to where they were killed while performing a mission.[9]

On June 19, 1959, nearly eight months following the crash of the Vulcan bomber, the body of copilot Flt. Lt. Peacock was recovered from the waters of the Detroit River.[10]

With the removal of wreckage and the rebuilding of homes, the area in which the crash occurred quickly rebounded. Largely due to the fact that there was no loss of life among those living in the area, the episode quickly faded from the headlines. Today, with the passage of time, the crash of the Vulcan bomber during that autumn afternoon of 1958 is a largely forgotten episode in Detroit's history.

Following the crash in Michigan, British bombers continued their regular deployments to North America. As one of Britain's primary means of projecting power during the early years of the Cold War, the Avro Vulcan received a number of upgrades as improvements became available. [11]

The first production example of an improved variant of the Vulcan, designated as the B.Mk.2, took to the air on August 19, 1958. Among other improvements, the wingspan of this model was increased to 111-feet, or a 12-foot increase when compared to the B.Mk.1. The increased wing area, combined with more powerful engines, allowed for a 5,000 foot increase in operational altitude. This model began arriving in RAF squadrons on July 1, 1960.[12]

By the mid-1960s, the increasing sophistication of Soviet air defense systems forced the Vulcan to adopt low-level attack profiles in an effort to evade radar detection, and thus improve its survivability in hostile airspace. To reflect this switch in tactics, the Vulcan fleet's original white anti-flash color scheme was replaced by a gray and green camouflage pattern.

During the 1960s, a number of Vulcan B.Mk.2s received modifications to carry the Blue Steel nuclear-armed missile. This weapon had a range of in excess of 100 miles, and remained in operational service until the early 1970s before being withdrawn.

By the 1970s, the focus of Britain's nuclear deterrent had shifted to its ballistic missile submarine force. Despite this, the Vulcan remained in front line service with the RAF, serving in the conventional strike and reconnaissance roles. By the final years of that decade, however, it was clear that the 1950s vintage bomber was nearing the end of its operational career.

Despite its increasing obsolescence, the Vulcan was routinely deployed to North America during this period, with the type making an occasional air show appearance. With its unique shape and ability to perform high angle-of-attack climbs from low altitude, the aging bomber was a popular attraction at such events.

For Chicago's 1978 Lakefront Festival Air Show, the Royal Air Force dispatched a Vulcan bomber belonging to the Bomber Command's No. 617 Squadron to take part in the flying display. This aircraft, serial number XL390, was a B.Mk.2 model that had been delivered to the RAF in July 1962, and was later fitted with more powerful engines and the capability to carry the Blue Steel missile.

With the air show scheduled for the weekend, Friday, August 11, was sanctioned as a practice day for the event's performers. With the actual flying displays taking place over Lake Michigan, participating aircraft were required to utilize local airports. On this occasion, the British Vulcan bomber was operating from the Glenview Naval Air Station, about 17 miles north of downtown Chicago.

Aboard XL908 as it taxied to the runway at Glenview to embark upon a rehearsal flight this particular Friday during the summer of 1978 was Flight Lt. Chris Edwards, commander; Flight Lt. Simon Farlow, copilot; Flight Lt. Jamie Hamilton, air electronics officer; and Flight Lt. Nigel Thomas, navigator.[13]

As the British jet bomber performed its takeoff roll, all appeared normal. This changed within a few moments as the Vulcan suddenly dove towards the ground before crashing into a landfill just north of the airfield. The massive fireball that resulted left little doubt as to the fate of the crew. Radio operators on the ground received no indication of any trouble

A Vulcan demonstrating its ability to conduct a steep climb upon taking off at an air show in 1984. (Defense Imagery)

from the pilots of the doomed jet.

Rescue workers arrived at the scene immediately following the accident. Working through smoke and flames, they were able to establish what witnesses to the crash had already surmised. All four of the RAF airmen aboard XL390 had perished when their jet burst into flames.

Witnesses on the ground reported that within moments of the Vulcan beginning its climb it appeared to stall at an altitude of approximately 400 feet before it began falling from the sky. When first beginning its final plunge, the nose of the jet was aimed towards a populated section in the community of Northbrook, Illinois. A few moments later, however, it appears that the pilot was able to regain some control of the plummeting jet as he managed to steer it towards the only open ground in the vicinity.[14]

The following excerpt concerning the crash is from a UPI news release that appeared in Elyria, Ohio's *The Chronicle-Telegram* on August 12, 1978:

> The pilot of a British Vulcan bomber, who died in a crash along with three crew members, apparently intentionally aimed the plane for a garbage dump to avoid hitting a residential area.
>
> "It would be a miracle in a way if he just landed there (in dump) accidentally," said John Egbert, chief of the naval station's public information office. "That is the only open area surrounding the naval center and it's entirely possible he was headed there to avoid a bigger tragedy."

As had occurred at Detroit some twenty years earlier, this crash occurred on a Friday and there were no casualties on the ground. Furthermore, as both accidents occurred in heavily populated areas it is remarkable that the loss of life was not much larger.

While the wreckage of XL390 was spread over a large portion of the landfill, the bodies of the unfortunate crew were quickly recovered by rescue workers. Searchers found one body nearly 100 yards from the main impact site, while another was located under a section of one of the craft's huge wings. The remains of the other two crewmembers were discovered within several feet of the Vulcan's wreckage.[15]

Scheduled to be withdrawn from active duty within a nearby timeframe, the Vulcan was nearing the end of its operational career with the Royal Air Force at the time of the 1978 disaster. In fact, this crash was the final occurrence in which an example of this 1950s era jet bomber was written off in an accident.

Interestingly, the only actual combat missions flown by the Vulcan bomber during its lengthy career took place in 1982 during the Falklands War, just prior to the type's retirement. Designated Operation Black Buck, these bombing missions, the longest in history at the time, saw the Vulcan attacking Argentine forces on the Falklands with conventional weapons. On two of the five attack missions that actually reached the Falklands, the attacking Vulcans employed the US supplied AGM-45 Shrike anti-radar missile, a weapon heretofore not part of the aircraft's armament.

Following the conclusion of the Falklands War, a small number of these bombers received modifications enabling them to operate as aerial refueling tankers. After faithfully serving in front-line service for twenty-eight years, the Vulcan was finally retired from operational service with the RAF in 1984. Including the two prototypes, 136 Vulcan bombers were built. Of these, 21 aircraft, or just over 15 percent of the total manufactured, were written off in crashes during the type's operational career.

Chapter Ten
"No...No!!"

It is the early morning hours of November 24, 1959 and people living in the neighborhoods bordering Chicago's Midway Airport had long grown accustomed to the constant drone of aircraft overhead as they arrive and depart what was currently the world's busiest airport. With Thanksgiving just two days away, the city is busy preparing for the upcoming holiday season. Although sunrise would not occur for nearly another hour and a half, the crew of a Lockheed L-1049H Super Constellation operated by Trans World Airlines (TWA) was preparing their aircraft for takeoff from the busy airfield. At 5:31 a.m., the four-engine cargo plane began its roll down the runway. After picking up sufficient speed, the nose of the airliner pitched slightly upwards and the 63 ton craft rose into the gloomy skies hovering over the second largest city in the United States.[1] Unbeknownst to the plane's crew, and those living near the airport, the onset of a minor engine problem a few seconds after takeoff would soon shatter the relative peacefulness of the autumn morning.

In June of 1939, Howard Hughes, the eccentric and colorful millionaire, visited the Lockheed Aircraft Company to urge the development of an airliner capable of flying nonstop across the continental United States. Hughes intended to place the aircraft into service with Transcontinental & Western Air (TWA), an airline in which he had recently gained a controlling interest.[2] To meet this requirement, Lockheed developed a 40-passenger airliner, designated as the Model 49 (L-049) Constellation, for which Hughes immediately placed an order for 40 examples.

By time the first prototype flew on January 9, 1943, however, America's entry into the Second World War had forced a halt to all commercial aircraft production in the United States. Although the U.S. Army Air Forces (USAAF) placed an order for 202 of these transports, designated as the C-69, very few would actually enter service prior to the end of the war.[3]

The Constellation received its Civil Aeronautics Administration (CAA) certification on December 11, 1945, this having followed initial deliveries of the aircraft to commercial carriers the previous month. Incorporating a tall undercarriage and triple tail configuration, the Lockheed Constellation became one the most widely recognizable piston-powered airliners ever produced. Appearing somewhat ungainly on the ground, the Constellation flew through the skies with a grace that few other aircraft have equaled, much less surpassed. To this day, the aircraft remains affectionately referred to as the "Connie."

On February 3, 1946, the Constellation entered service with Pan American Airways on its Bermuda route. Just three days later, Trans World Airlines placed this aircraft into operation on its transatlantic route between New York and Paris. In July of that year, British Overseas Airways (BOAC) inaugurated Constellation service between London and New York.[4]

Building upon the success of their four-engine airliner, Lockheed developed the L-1049 Super Constellation. Improvements included a fuselage stretched by 18 feet 4 inches, uprated Wright R-3350 engines, and a larger fuel capacity. Following the conversion of the original Constellation prototype to the L-1049 specification, this variant flew for the first time on October 13, 1950.

In regards to production figures, the most popular commercial Super Constellation variant was the L-1049G, which also represented the ultimate expression of this aircraft model in terms of performance characteristics. Able to accommodate up to 95 passengers, this model was fitted with four Wright R-3350-DA3 engines each of which was capable of generating 3,400 horsepower. To increase the range of the aircraft, auxiliary fuel tanks could be mounted on the wingtips. With a maximum load of fuel, the L-1049G had a range of 5,100 miles.[5]

The first G model flew on December 12, 1954, with production examples entering service with Northwest Airlines early the following year. Based upon the G model, Lockheed developed a convertible passenger/cargo variant designated as the L-1049H.

A L-1049H Constellation restored as a "Super G" by the Kansas City, Missouri based National Airline History Museum. (Defense Imagery)

Capable of carrying a maximum payload of 24,293 pounds, production of this model totaled 53 examples.

At 2:16 a.m. on the morning of November 24, 1959, a Lockheed L-1049H operated by TWA touched down at Chicago's Midway Airport to conclude a flight originating at New York City.[6] Registered as N102R, this Super Constellation had been in service for nearly two and a half years following its completion by the manufacturer on June 6, 1957.

After arriving at Chicago, a scheduled crew change would take place prior to the aircraft's departure for Los Angeles. In charge of the crew coming aboard was Captain Claude W. Helwig, whom at age forty was a fourteen-year veteran pilot with TWA. During his career, Helwig had amassed 12,467 total flight hours, of which 1,670 were attained with the Lockheed Constellation. Captain Helwig was certified to operate the L-1049G model of the four-engine aircraft on July 3, 1956.

Joining Captain Helwig was First Officer Delmas E. Watters, age 36. Delmas had been with TWA since October 27, 1952, and had some 3,919 hours aboard the Constellation, a figure that represented well over half of his total flight experience of 6,285 hours. The final member of the crew was Flight Engineer Aerion L. Auge, Jr., whom at age 35 was the youngest of the three persons aboard. First employed by the airline on May 4, 1953, the flight engineer had racked up an impressive 5,100 hours worth of flight time as an engineer aboard Constellation equipment.

All three crewmembers had been off duty since the previous Friday (November 20). Deciding to spend the weekend at their homes in California, rather than in Chicago, each had traveled home aboard company flights. On Monday (November 23), with the weekend now over, the crewmembers began making their way back to Chicago aboard a variety of flights. First to return was First Officer Watters when he arrived at Midway at 7:20 a.m. before checking into a local hotel. Captain Helwig arrived at the airfield at 4:45 p.m., later signing in at the airline's crew lounge at 9:40 p.m., before beginning a rest period. Arriving at O'Hare International Airport at 9:15 p.m., Flight Engineer Auge was the final member of the crew to return to Chicago. After commuting through the city to reach Midway Airport, the flight engineer finally checked into the TWA lounge at 11:45 that evening.[7]

By two o'clock on the morning of November 24, all three crewmembers had received instructions to fly N102R to Los Angeles with a load of freight as Flight 595. Although originally scheduled to depart Midway at 3:10 a.m., the flight's departure was delayed by two hours and twenty minutes due to a breakdown in the ground loading equipment.

With the exception of a minor discrepancy with a spark plug in each of the Nos. 1, 2, and 4 engines, the incoming flight crew reported that N102R's flight from New York as being uneventful. After reviewing the spark plug issue, ground maintenance personnel, as well as Flight Engineer Auge, agreed there was no need to change the affected plugs and that the aircraft was airworthy for the flight to Los Angeles.[8]

Aboard the aircraft was approximately 18,000 pounds of cargo, which included 4,000 pounds of mail destined for the Los Angeles area.[9] Among the items strapped to the floor in the TWA plane's fuselage was a 5,880-pound jet engine.

After filing an instrument flight rules (IFR) flight plan, the crew of Flight 595 started the aircraft's engines shortly after 5 o'clock in the morning. At 5:20 a.m., Lloyd Harold, the controller stationed in Midway's tower, instructed Captain Helwig to taxi to runway 31L (left) in preparation for departure.[10] Eleven minutes later, Flight 595 was given its air traffic control (ATC) clearance for the cross-country flight to Los Angeles and cleared for takeoff.

Within moments of receiving its clearance, the crew of the TWA cargo plane acknowledged the control tower's instructions and began the takeoff roll. To the personnel working in Midway's tower, the takeoff of N102R appeared normal. One minute and thirteen seconds after beginning down the runway, the tower received a routine transmission from the departing plane stating that it was beginning a left turn in accordance with instructions given prior to takeoff.

Seven seconds later, Captain Helwig transmitted, "Uh, Midway tower, TWA 595. We just got a fire bell on Number 2. We're coming back in. We've shut it [engine No. 2] down." Responding to the emergency, the controller first gave the flight permission to land on runway 4R, and subsequently on 31L, the latter being chosen by Captain Helwig to land his crippled plane.[11] Following this, Controller Harold inquired whether rescue equipment would be necessary. Confident that the engine trouble was minor in nature, the crew of Flight 595 rejected this offer as being unnecessary. Midway tower then asked Captain Helwig if he wanted to conduct an instrument landing system (ILS) or a visual flight rules (VFR) approach, to which the TWA pilot replied, "I think we'll make it VFR OK."

An ILS approach to runway 31L would have required the

Constellation to climb to an altitude of 1,500 feet above sea level, or about 900 feet above the elevation of Midway Airport. After climbing to this altitude, the airliner would begin its descent to runway 31L after passing over the Kedzie radio beacon located 3.3 nautical miles from the end of the runway. As the prevailing cloud base over the airfield that morning was at approximately 600 feet, it would have been necessary for the aircraft to climb into the overcast in order to perform an ILS approach. Perhaps, this factor most heavily influenced Captain Helwig's decision to conduct a VFR approach to the runway. While this decision prevented losing sight of the ground by climbing into the overcast, it also made it necessary to fly the aircraft at an altitude of just 400 to 600 feet above the ground during its return to the airport.[12]

Two minutes and forty-seven seconds after taking off, the crew of the TWA cargo plane acknowledged its clearance to land on runway 31L. During the time elapsed, the aircraft had nearly completed a left handed circuit in order to line back up on the runway from which it had departed. During the left turn onto its final approach heading, however, witnesses on the ground watched as the lumbering cargo plane suddenly entered into a bank angle exceeding 45 degrees.

Rapidly losing what precious little altitude it had remaining, the crew of the Constellation made a desperate attempt to get the wings level and bring the nose up to avoid crashing into the neighborhoods below. Though the pilots succeeded in getting the wings level, and the nose pointed slightly upwards, the aircraft's descent rate continued until it crashed into a row of houses three blocks southeast of the airport's perimeter. At the same moment, the controller in the tower shouted, "No...No!!" over the radio in a spontaneous reaction to what he had just witnessed.

The crash occurred at 5:35 a.m., a time established by the Commonwealth Edison Company of Chicago as the moment when a local power failure occurred simultaneously with Flight 595 hitting the power lines.[13] Besides the three crewmembers aboard the aircraft, the crash also killed eight people on the ground. Coming down near 64th Street and Cicero Avenue, wreckage and fuel from the TWA plane set ten dwellings on fire.[14]

Awoken by the crash, Fire Lt. Harold Prohaska hurried to the crash site, thus making him one of the first rescuers to arrive on the scene. In doing so, he came across one of the pilots still strapped in his seat, some 30 to 40 feet away from the burning wreckage. Unable to detect a pulse, Prohaska soon realized that he could nothing for the pilot. During the early minutes following the crash, the fire lieutenant also came across the body of another man lying on a sidewalk, and tried to reach a pair of burning bungalows before being forced back by the intensity of the inferno engulfing them.[15]

Firefighters fought through the early morning hours to get the flames under control. Indicating that only four persons on the ground had been killed, early reports from the crash site were, as can be expected, sketchy at best. As the day progressed, however, the death toll was revised as accurate information became available. By late that afternoon, it had been firmly established that there were actually seven people killed on the ground, with one still listed as missing.

A USAF VC-121E shown with its landing gear and flaps extended. This configuration is similar to that flown by the crew of N102R during their final turn to line up on Midway's runway 31L. (Defense Imagery)

Among the early victims identified were Mr. Diean Nichols and his wife, Jo Anne, whom were both employed at Midway Airport by the Chicago Helicopter Airways.[16] On the morning of the accident, Frank Costello, a coworker, had seen the fires from the crash on his way to the airfield. After the married couple did not show up for work, Mr. Costello became suspicious and began searching for the pair. After arriving at the morgue later that day, he was able to make a positive identification of his coworker's bodies.[17]

Other victims on the ground included Mrs. Gisella Petrisco and her five-month-old son, Mark, Elizabeth Mehalov, age 44, and her son George Jr., 18, and daughter Betty Ann, 16.[18] After being listed as missing throughout the day of the crash, the final victim, Mrs. Dorothea Rak, age 41, was finally located by rescuers as evening closed in. Recovered from the basement of a demolished house next to where she had resided, the Police surmised that the force of the cargo plane's crash had thrown the unfortunate woman from her own home into the structure next door.[19] In addition to those killed, at least eleven others were injured, three of which were still reported as being in critical condition the day following the accident.[20]

As often happens in such disasters, a number of stories emerged of individuals that narrowly escaped serious injury or death. One such tale involved the family of Thomas Fracassi, which occupied one of the homes hit by the plummeting aircraft. While the crash caved in part of the roof into one of the bedrooms, Thomas Fracassi, age 31, his wife, and three children were able to flee their burning home. Although all five members of the family managed to escape with their lives, two of the children were injured.[21]

On the day of the accident, the crash of Flight 595 became a front-page feature in newspapers across the nation. In several periodicals, the story maintained this status throughout the balance of the week. Perhaps the best summation of the published remarks of residents living in the neighborhood in which the accident occurred was the following passage that appeared in a number of newspapers the day of the accident: "It seemed like the end of the world."

The Civil Aeronautics Board received notification of the crash of Flight 595 at 6:05 a.m., November 24, 1959, and in accordance with its established procedures immediately initiated an investigation into the accident. Within twenty-four hours of the disaster, four teams of investigators had arrived on the scene to begin the tedious process of piecing together what had taken place.[22]

By interviewing a number of witnesses, investigators were able to reconstruct an approximate flight path representing that flown by the doomed TWA cargo plane during its brief flight. The elliptical flight path established that the aircraft covered approximately eight statute miles from its takeoff roll to the site of the crash, during which time Captain Helwig never flew more than two miles distant from Midway Airport.

Several witnesses, including those who were in the control tower at the time of the accident, stated that the airliner entered into a bank in excess of 45 degrees during the left turn to line up for its final approach to the runway. During this maneuver, the Constellation rapidly lost altitude until nearly leveling out just before striking the trees and structures below.

Investigators combing through the wreckage found that the nose and two main landing gear assemblies were in their retracted positions. Of these, only the right main gear was in its "locked" configuration. It was determined that the aircraft's wing flaps were extended by approximately 13 inches, or 24 percent of their full range of movement, at the time of crash. When recovered, the wing flap control lever in the cockpit was found positioned one-eighth of an inch aft of its full forward position for flap retraction.

As the crew reported having received an engine fire warning on engine No. 2, this powerplant received extra scrutiny. While an examination of this engine revealed that the crew of Flight 595 had activated its fire extinguisher, investigators could find no evidence of an in-flight fire. Impact forces of the crash and the subsequent fire prevented any testing of the fire warning system of this engine. It was theorized, however, that since the crew had declined the offer to have emergency equipment standing by upon their landing, they had already concluded that there was no actual fire in engine No. 2.

Finding no evidence of a structural failure or a shifting of the aircraft's cargo, the investigation expanded to include a flight test program. This was performed by the aircraft's manufacturer, the Lockheed Corporation, at Los Angeles. Simulating conditions experienced by Flight 595 as closely as possible, these flights established that warnings of impending stall were apparent to the pilot, and that recoveries could be performed with loss of no more than 200 feet of altitude. On one of these test runs, however, the pilot placed the Constellation into a bank of 42 degrees and allowed the airspeed to drop to 108 knots (124 mph). During this particular test, a high sink rate developed prior to the aircraft entering the stall buffet zone. With insufficient power to keep the four engine aircraft in level flight, a loss of several hundred feet was required to gain enough airspeed to recover from the descent. The pilot flying the test aircraft during this instance described the condition as being on the backside of the power curve.[23]

With the fire warning on engine No. 2 occurring so early in the flight, investigators speculated that the crew had left the wing flaps extended at their takeoff setting of 60 percent, with the landing gear most likely being extended on the downwind portion of the traffic pattern. As the aircraft began to make its final approach to runway 31L, a sharp turn was necessary to avoid overshooting the landing strip's centerline. While attempting to perform this maneuver, it was theorized that Captain Helwig made too sharp of a bank for the heavily loaded plane operating at low altitude on three engines. At some point during this turn, the captain must have decided to perform a "go -around" and called for the gear to be retracted. For some unexplained reason, however, it appears that during this same time the flap control lever was also repositioned to retract the wing flaps. Combined with the aircraft's low altitude and high sink rate, the loss of lift concurrent with the retraction of the flaps made a crash unavoidable.

On May 12, 1961, nearly a year and a half following the crash of Flight 595, the CAB issued its findings. In this report, the investigators placed the blame of the crash directly upon the aircraft's crew. Taken from this report, the following excerpt states the probable cause of the crash:

> The Board determines the probable cause of this accident to be the maneuvering of the aircraft in a manner that caused it to develop an excessive rate of sink while in the turn to final approach.

The crash of Flight 595 was the second accident to occur during 1959 involving a cargo plane attempting to land at Midway Airport. On March 15 of that year, a Convair CV-240 operated by American Airlines crashed in a rail yard 1 ½ miles southeast of the airport. While the aircraft was destroyed in the accident, both of the pilots aboard were able to walk away after suffering only minor injuries.[24]

After the wreckage of the TWA Flight 595 disaster was cleared away, life began to return normal in the community bordering

The L-1649 Starliner was the ultimate variant of Lockheed's Constellation design. First flying in 1956, this aircraft was eclipsed within a few years by jet-powered airliners. (NASA)

Midway Airport. The vast majority of people living in the area, many of whom worked at the airfield, were undeterred by the crash and remained living in the area. Following the opening of O'Hare International Airport in 1955, air traffic began declining at Midway. After a resurgence of air traffic at Midway during the mid to late sixties, all major carriers ceased operations at the airport in 1973 due in part to a nationwide oil shortage. After 1978, however, Deregulation rekindled interest in Midway, leading to an upward swing in the amount of air traffic at the airport. During 2012, there were 249,913 aircraft movements at Midway, a number that includes both commercial and general aviation aircraft.[25]

By the time of the Chicago accident, the Constellation had been out of production for over a year. The last commercial variant of this aircraft developed by Lockheed was the L-1649A Starliner, of which only 44 were produced.[26] The first of these flew on October 11, 1956, with TWA inaugurating commercial service with the type during June of 1957.[27] By this time, however, the dawn of jet travel had arrived and with it the end of the line for aircraft such as the Lockheed Constellation and its chief rival, the Douglas DC-6/7 series. As such, the Constellation was removed from regular passenger service in North America during the 1960s. Although the type would soldier on for a number of years with air cargo carriers, by the mid-1970s only a handful of Constellations remained in regular airline service worldwide.

Besides the Constellations it constructed for the commercial market, Lockheed used the design to produce a wide range of variants for the military. The U.S. Air Force and Navy used these aircraft in a number of roles, including some examples that served as airborne early warning (AEW) aircraft during the Vietnam War. By the late 1970s, most of the Constellation variants acquired by the U.S. military had been replaced by more modern types.

The only other commercial airliner built by Lockheed during the 1950s was the turboprop powered L-188 Electra. Although this aircraft was later used as the basis for the highly successful P-3 Orion anti-submarine patrol aircraft, it enjoyed only mediocre success in the commercial market. Lockheed would go on to produce only one further large passenger aircraft, the L-1011 Tristar, before ceasing production of commercial airliners in 1984. In 1995, Lockheed merged with Martin Marietta, thus becoming Lockheed Martin.

Today, a small number of Constellations remain in flyable

condition. Mostly kept in the air through the hard work of volunteers, many of these aircraft can be found making the air show circuit on an annual basis. Besides the airworthy airframes, there are many examples, of various variants, preserved in museums. Unfortunately, there is also a number of Constellations abandoned in various spots around the world, their days of usefulness appearing to have now come to an end.

Chapter Eleven
"There was a sudden orange flash..."

As a light breeze blew in from across the waters of Lake Michigan during the early evening hours of August 16, 1965, citizens living in Chicago's North Shore area were getting some relief from a brutally hot day. Shortly after 9:20 p.m., however, the darkening skies over the freshwater lake suddenly turned orange as an explosion lit up the horizon. Even as the fireball disappeared a few seconds later, a rumbling noise was heard cascading from offshore. Although not realizing it at the time, those observing this event had just witnessed the first crash of a Boeing 727.

In February 1956, some two years before its Model 707 entered service, Boeing began design work on a short/medium haul airliner that was to be designated as the 727. Before finalizing the basic design for the new jetliner in the autumn of 1959, engineers at Boeing had studied a number of powerplant configurations before adopting a three-engine layout.[1] This arrangement consisted of two engines mounted in pods at the rear of the fuselage, with a third engine installed at the rear of the fuselage under the tail. The third engine was supplied air by a duct extending forward from the base of the vertical stabilizer, thus giving the aircraft an easily identifiable profile.

The design of the 727 shared a high degree of commonality with its immediate predecessor, the 707, one such feature being an identical upper fuselage lobe. This permitted the use of similar cabin and cockpit arrangements, thus saving Boeing approximately \$3 million in tooling and jig costs.[2]

To provide the 727 with excellent short-field performance capabilities, engineers developed a highly innovative wing design equipped with both high-lift and lift-dump devices. Incorporating the most advanced aerodynamics developed for a commercial aircraft up to that time, the Boeing 727 embarked on its maiden flight on February 9, 1963.

Powered by three Pratt & Whitney JT8D-1 turbofan engines, each of which was capable of generating 14,000 pounds of thrust, the 727 combined a nimble performance with good fuel economy characteristics. Capable of carrying up to a maximum of 129 passengers, the 727-100 had a wingspan of 108 feet and an overall length of 133 feet 2 inches.[3]

Envisioned to operate from airfields lacking extensive ground servicing equipment, this aircraft was equipped with an onboard auxiliary power unit (APU) and a ventral staircase that extended from the rear fuselage, below and in front of the tail mounted engine.

Confident that orders would be forthcoming, Boeing's management approved the production of the 727 in August 1960. The first firm orders for the plane did not materialize until December of that year, when United Airlines ordered twenty examples, while taking options on an additional twenty, and Eastern Air Lines committed to the purchase of forty aircraft. Having received its first 727 in October 1963, Eastern inaugurated passenger service with the type on February 1, 1964 with scheduled services between Miami and Philadelphia. Five days later, United also began 727 operations when it placed its new trijet into service on a number of its routes.[4]

On June 3, 1965, Boeing delivered a 727-22, registered as N7036U, to United Airlines.[5] Just over ten weeks later, on August 16, 1965, this aircraft was operating as Flight 389 when it departed New York's LaGuardia Airport bound for Chicago's O'Hare International Airport. Earlier that day, N7036U had arrived at LaGuardia following a cross-country trip originating at Los Angeles, California with intermediate stops at Sacramento, California; Reno, Nevada; Denver, Colorado; and Chicago, Illinois. Spanning the length of the nation, such a route illustrates an operational role in which the 727 was well suited to perform.

The flight crew for Flight 389 arrived at LaGuardia one hour before the aircraft's scheduled departure. In command on this flight, and employed by United since February 1946, was 42 year -old Captain Melville W. Towle. During his career, Towle had accumulated an impressive 17,142 flight hours, and besides holding a type rating with the 727, he was also qualified to operate the DC-3, DC-4, and Vickers Viscount. At the time of this flight, however, he only had 59 hours of experience as a pilot -in-command of the Boeing 727.

Hired on February 27, 1956, First Officer Roger M. Whitezell, age 34, had been with United for just over nine years. He had completed 363 out of his total 8,466 flight hours operating the 727. Rounding out the flight crew was Second Officer Maurice L. Femmer, whom, at age 26, was also the youngest member of the flight crew. Femmer had only been with United since April of 1964, but since then had recorded 649 flight hours with the airline.

United Airlines was one of two launch customers for the Boeing 727. This photograph illustrates the type's engine placement. (Author's Collection)

With twenty-four passengers aboard, N7036U departed LaGuardia at 7:52 p.m. that summer evening bound for Chicago.[6] With the cabin of the jetliner only filled to approximately one-quarter of its capacity, the three stewardesses aboard the flight could look forward to a quiet evening. Consisting of Phyllis M. Rickert, Sandra H. Fuhrer, and Jeneal G. Beaver, the cabin crew had previously joined the aircraft at Chicago on its eastbound trip to LaGuardia. While both Rickert and Fuhrer had been with United since November 1964, Beaver had been with the airline for just over five months. With her two comrades just nearing their twenty-first birthdays, Phyllis Rickert, at twenty-two, was oldest of the three stewardesses.

Nineteen minutes after departing LaGuardia, the crew radioed ground control to report Flight 389 having reached its intended cruising altitude of 35,000 feet. At 9:02 p.m., the eastbound 727 came under control of the Chicago Air Route Traffic Control

Center (ARTCC). After establishing contact with that facility, Flight 389 received clearance to proceed towards O'Hare at its present flight level. Just one minute later, however, the controller directed the United jetliner to begin a descent to 24,000 feet.

At 9:06 p.m., the ARTCC controller instructed Flight 389 to continue its descent to 14,000 feet and informed the pilots that the current altimeter setting for O'Hare was 29.90 inches. After acknowledging this message, the crew reported passing through 28,000 feet. At this altitude, the Boeing trijet entered a layer of clouds, in which it would remain until descending below approximately 8,000 feet.

Even as it continued its descent through the clouds at 9:09 p.m., the Chicago ARTCC instructed the jetliner to change its radio frequencies. A few moments later, the controller received a message, most likely transmitted by Captain Towle, reporting the descending aircraft as having passed through 26,000 feet along with confirming the descent clearance to 14,000 feet. This message proved to be the last altitude information received from the 727's flight crew. At 9:11 p.m., ground control cleared Flight 389 to continue its descent down to 6,000 feet.

As the jetliner neared the western shore of Lake Michigan, it became the responsibility of Chicago Approach Control (ORD). This transfer took place at 9:18 p.m., and one minute later, the approach controller instructed Flight 389 to maintain 6,000 feet. The controller also advised the crew of the 727 that the instrument landing system on runway 14R was operable at O'Hare, and that the current barometric altimeter setting at the airport was 29.93 inches. Reading back his instructions, Captain

Towle repeated the altimeter setting incorrectly. After the controller pointed out this mistake, Captain Towle read it back correctly. This message, which ended a few seconds after 9:20 p.m., was the last transmission ever received from N7036U.

For some reason, no one will ever be sure, the pilots of the 727 never leveled off at 6,000 feet, and continued their descent unabated. In spite of the fact that that airliner had broken through the cloud base and visibility was at seven to ten miles, the crew did not notice the aircraft descending below its assigned altitude. Furthermore, at the time of Captain Towle's final transmission to approach control, as investigators would later determine, Flight 389 was already below 3,000 feet. As the level of Lake Michigan rises 577 feet above sea level, and the airliner's rate of descent was approximately 2,500 feet per minute, there would have been approximately sixty seconds between the last radio message received from the 727 and its impact with the water.

At 9:20 p.m., in almost level flight, the right wing of the Boeing 727 struck the surface of Lake Michigan. As the wing dug into the water, it forced the aircraft to rotate to the right. Almost simultaneously, the lower forward section of the fuselage and the undersides of the wing struck the water as the breakup sequence began. When N7036U struck the water, its landing gear, flaps, leading-edge slats, and spoilers were all in their retracted positions. The impact killed all 6 crewmembers and 24 passengers instantly and triggered an explosion and fire, which was clearly visible to those on shore and in boats in the surrounding area. When interviewed by a reporter following the incident, one witness, a lifeguard at a Chicago beach remarked:

"There was a sudden orange flash on the northeastern horizon like [the] break of day, and then a deep rumbling sound."[7]

Many witnesses reported seeing a fireball above the surface of the lake, moments before the crash. Reports such as these, combined with the suddenness of the plane's disappearance, fueled speculation that there may have been an in-flight explosion prior to the 727 plunging into the cold waters of Lake Michigan. In part, the possibility that an explosion had occurred aboard airliner, prompted the FBI to review the passenger list in New York to determine whether anyone aboard the ill-fated flight had made any substantial life insurance policy purchases.[8]

Immediately following the crash of Flight 389, several boats began converging on the area in which the plane vanished. This flotilla included craft belonging to the U.S. Navy and Coast Guard, along with those of private ownership as well. Although the weather was calm at the time of the crash, a storm during the early hours of the next morning caused the lake to become choppy.[9]

After receiving notification of the crash, the Civil Aeronautics Board (CAB) initiated an investigation into the disaster. Dispatched from Washington D.C., the team of CAB investigators arrived in Chicago to take charge of the inquiry. Faced with the formidable challenge of piecing together what had occurred, the investigative team's task was complicated further by the aircraft's wreckage being lost somewhere in the depths of Lake Michigan.

On the day following the crash, a team of FBI agents arrived in Chicago to assist other agencies involved in the investigation. Although the participation of FBI personnel is a routine aspect of any such air disaster, the sudden, and unexplained, loss of the United 727 presented the possibility that someone may have sabotaged the aircraft prior to its last flight.[10] Besides its possible role in any criminal investigation, the FBI was also prepared to assist in the identification of the crash victims.

At 6:30 a.m. on August 17, 1965, some nine hours after the crash, the first pieces of debris from the missing plane were sighted 16 miles due east of Waukegan, Illinois. Consisting of various articles, this wreckage included a five-foot section of fiberglass and several pieces of luggage. The discovery was made by the U.S. Coast Guard cutter *Woodbine,* which was arriving on the scene to take command of the search. Concurrent with this finding were reports of oil washing ashore at Highland Park, a suburb of Chicago about ten miles north of the city limits.[11]

Even as the *Woodbine* was retrieving the initial pieces of debris, a helicopter searching an area of Lake Michigan about 25 miles east of Highland Park spotted the first victims found from the crash.[12] After being notified of this sighting, the *Woodbine* recovered four bodies from the rough waters of Lake Michigan, while the 110-foot U.S. Coast Guard harbor tug *Arundel* retrieved a fifth. These victims, along with a sixth, were taken to a temporary morgue established in the gymnasium of the Highland Park High School.[13] One of the bodies recovered at this time was subsequently identified as Captain Melville Towle.

Among those killed in the crash of Flight 389 was Clarence N. Sayen, a businessman from Seattle, Washington. Mr. Sayen had previously served as president of the Air Line Pilots Association for nearly eleven years. During his time in that capacity,

Clarence Sayen had campaigned incessantly for air safety legislation.[14]

In the days immediately following the disaster, poor weather impeded the search for clues. These conditions restricted the effectiveness of the two helicopters and one fixed-wing aircraft assigned to the recovery operation. Within two days, however, searchers had identified the general location in which they believed the passenger jet had crashed, and cordoned off an area of the lake to expedite the recovery of debris.[15]

During the first three days of the search operation, several thousand pounds of floating debris was recovered, much of this being taken aboard the cutter *Woodbine*. After this, however, searchers retrieved little else from Lake Michigan until the discovery of the wreckage site on September 2, 1965. The wreck of the 727 was found to be lying in approximately 250 feet of water 19 miles due east of Lake Forest, Illinois. This location put the aircraft some 30 miles northeast of it intended destination, O'Hare International Airport.

The onset of winter brought upon the suspension of recovery operations on December 21, 1965. By this time, searchers had reclaimed approximately 82 percent of the aircraft's weight in debris, and recovered all of the victims of the crash.

The following summer witnessed a resumption of search and recovery operations. With an emphasis being placed upon locating components of the aircraft's flight data recorder (FDR) and missing portions of the No. 3 engine, the second search of the submerged wreckage began on June 17, 1966. The only items belonging to the FDR recovered during the initial search were two pieces of its casing. Meanwhile, the recorder's tape remained lost in the depths of the freshwater lake. After bringing an additional 1,500 pounds of wreckage to the surface, none of which belonged to the flight data recorder, the second search of the wreck site concluded.[16]

The failure to locate the elusive FDR tape frustrated the efforts by investigators to unravel the mystery. This disappointment was further compounded by the fact that N7036U was not equipped with a cockpit voice recorder (CVR). The absence of any hard evidence forced the investigation to examine a number of scenarios. As no other aircraft were reported missing, one of the easiest theories to discount was the possibility of a midair collision. As the recovered wreckage bore no signs of in-flight explosion and indicated the aircraft was in working order when it impacted the water, investigators were also able to rule out the bomb theory.

As examiners continued their probe of the wreckage, they continued to rule out other possible causes for the crash. Pathological and toxicology testing found nothing indicative of preexisting medical conditions or pre-crash incapacitation among any of the three members of the flight crew. With the aircraft's air conditioning ducts showing no sign of smoke, investigators also determined that there was no fire aboard the aircraft prior to the crash.

The examination of the wreckage also concluded that there were no malfunctions in the aircraft's electrical and hydraulic systems. Furthermore, all three engines were found to have been functioning normally up to the point of the 727 striking the surface of Lake Michigan. A review of N7036U's short history revealed a number of write-ups concerning the aircraft's autopilot system, including some work done just one day before the crash. As the nature of these discrepancies did not interfere with the control of the aircraft, they were considered as more of a nuisance to flight crews rather than a threat to the safety of the airliner. Examiners were able to obtain one useful piece of information from the aircraft's air data computer. This indicated an airspeed of 200-210 knots (230-242 mph) when electrical power was lost at the time of the crash.

To determine the weather conditions experienced by the crew of Flight 389 as it descended over Lake Michigan, investigators interviewed the crew of a Boeing 707 that was flying 30 miles behind the doomed airliner. The captain of this aircraft testified that after descending from a flight level of 28,000 feet, his aircraft broke through the cloud layer at an altitude of between 8,000 and 10,000 feet after encountering areas of light turbulence and precipitation. It was estimated that when the 707 descended through the cloud base it was approximately 15-20 miles offshore, thus placing it within the same general vicinity in which Flight 389 had vanished just minutes earlier. The captain of the 707 reported that the visibility after passing through the clouds was "fuzzy and unclear." In his testimony, the first officer stated that while it was hazy, he could see the water below. Both pilots reported that after breaking through the layer of clouds, lights on the shoreline were clearly visible.[17]

The investigation into the loss of Flight 389 benefited greatly from radar track information provided by the U.S Air Force Air Defense Command's Semi-Automatic Ground Environment (SAGE) system. Responsible for monitoring the airspace of North America to defend against enemy bomber attack, this

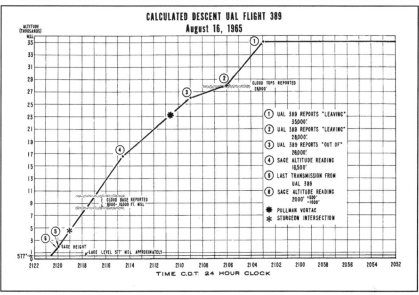

A chart created by the National Transportation Safety Board during the investigation into the crash of Flight 389. (NTSB)

radar network tracked the United 727 as it neared its destination on two separate occasions.

The Air Defense Command provided the investigation with two separate altitude readings for Flight 389 from the SAGE data. Recorded at 9:14:36 p.m., just six minutes before the crash, the first reading indicated that the 727 was at an altitude of 16,500 feet. The second reading, generated at 9:19:54 p.m., registered the descending jetliner at an altitude estimated at just 2,000 feet.[18]

Using the SAGE data, the crash investigators were able to establish two important facets of the last few minutes of Flight 389. First, the data provided evidence that the 727 was descending at a rate of approximately 2,500 feet per minute during the last few minutes of the flight. Secondly, the pilots of

117

the airliner made no effort to arrest their descent after reaching their altitude clearance limit of 6,000 feet. Taking place during the time that Captain Towle was receiving clearance from approach control to maintain 6,000 feet, the second SAGE altitude reading proved to be very significant to the crash investigation. Furthermore, it was during this final communication with the 727, that Captain Towle initially read back the incorrect altimeter setting for O'Hare, a mistake caught and corrected by the ground controller.

The reasons for the crew of Flight 389 allowing their aircraft to descend below its assigned altitude have never been fully determined. The airspace around Chicago is one of the busiest in the United States, therefore it is possible that in their efforts to maintain a lookout for other aircraft, the crew were distracted from monitoring their instruments.

Another possible factor involves the effectiveness of the three-

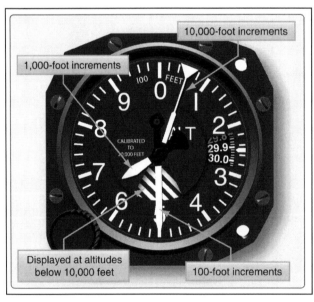

A graphic representation of a three-pointer altimeter, the type installed in the aircraft involved in the crash of Flight 389. Eight months before the accident, a research program conducted by the US Navy demonstrated the susceptibility of this type of gauge being misread by pilots.

pointer altimeter system installed in N7036U. As the name implies, an aircraft's altitude is presented on the display dial by three needles, or pointers. Eight months before the crash of Flight 389, the Naval Research Laboratory in Washington D. C. concluded a study comparing the effectiveness of four different altimeter displays. The altimeter types evaluated were the counter-pointer, counter-drum-pointer, drum-pointer, and three-pointer. Tests conducted during this program revealed that the three-pointer system was consistently the poorest performer of the four altimeters evaluated. As part of the program, a group of 18 pilots made 1,080 readings of each altimeter type. During these tests, the pilots misread the best performing altimeter, the counter-pointer, on only 7 occasions. In contrast, the three-pointer altimeter, the type available to Captain Towle and First Officer Whitezell, was misread in 80 instances during the same round of tests.[19]

The deficiencies of the three-pointer display led to speculation that the crew misinterpreted their altimeter readings, possibly misreading the instrument by 10,000 feet, thus allowing the airliner to descend below its clearance altitude of 6,000 feet. Such a mistake would have resulted in the 727 crashing into the surface of the lake. In light of no evidence of mechanical failure or crew incapacitation, such an error provides one the best explanations for the disaster.

Every crash investigator dreads an accident in which no probable cause can be established. While investigating the crash of Flight 389, however, the investigators faced just such a dilemma. Following an extensive period of testing and evaluation, the National Transportation Safety Board (NTSB)

In service until 2002, the Boeing 727 enjoyed a long operational career with United Airlines. Here, a 727-222 is shown in the airline's livery during early 1969. (Author's Collection)

published the investigation's findings on December 19, 1967.[20] In its report, the NTSB related an array of detailed information, none of which was identifiable as the accident's proverbial "smoking gun." Lacking any hard evidence, no probable cause could be determined as having led to the accident. Summing up the entire investigation, the final report included the following sentence:

> The Board is unable to determine the reason for the aircraft not being leveled off at its assigned altitude of 6,000 feet.

Meanwhile, Boeing continued to achieve success with its 727 design. Sales of this aircraft were such that by April 1967, only a little over three years after the type's first commercial flight, it had become the most widely used jet airliner in the world. In the same month that Flight 389 crashed into Lake Michigan, Boeing announced a stretched version of this aircraft. Designated as the 727-200, this model featured a fuselage 20 feet longer than that of the 727-100. Flying for the first time on July 27, 1967, the 727-200 became the definitive model of Boeing's trijet.[21]

In the early 1980s, Boeing introduced the 727's intended replacement, the 757, a twin-engine aircraft that shared little in common with the trijet other than an identical fuselage cross-section. Boeing delivered the final 727 to Federal Express on September 18, 1984, thus ending a twenty-two year production run. By that time, the aerospace giant had manufactured 1,832 examples of this aircraft, making it best selling commercial jetliner up to that time.[22]

Chapter Twelve
See and Avoid

Flight 853 was continuing its descent into the Weir Cook Municipal Airport, just outside of Indianapolis, Indiana. Belonging to Allegheny Airlines this aircraft, a McDonnell Douglas DC-9, had made numerous flights into this destination during its career without incident and there was no reason to believe that this instance would be any exception. Unseen, and to the right, of the jetliner as it descended through a layer of broken clouds on this particular day was a small Piper Cherokee traveling on its own intended course. The date is September 9, 1969 and in moments, all those aboard these two flying machines were to become the victims of a series of events that had conspired against them.

The McDonnell Douglas DC-9 was the result of a design effort to produce a jet-powered aircraft suited to operate on short routes. Previously, such operations had been the domain of piston and turboprop powered airliners. The introduction of the Boeing 707 and Douglas DC-8 during the late 1950s, however, enamored the flying public with the virtues of jet travel. While these two jet aircraft were capable of speeds far above what had previously been the norm with their piston-powered progenitors, their inability to operate out of smaller airports restricted the routes on which they could serve.

Shortly after the introduction of the DC-8, engineers at Douglas began development work on a jetliner tailored for operation on short and medium routes.[1] In 1959, this proposal, powered by four Pratt & Whitney turbojets, was presented to the airlines. Ultimately, many carriers, including United Airlines, rejected the design in favor of Boeing's 727. Douglas, however, realized that a market existed for an aircraft smaller than their rival's trijet, and began engineering work on such a project.

In 1962, after considering a number of configurations, Douglas approached the airlines with a completely new design powered by a pair of Pratt & Whitney JT8D turbojets mounted at the rear of the fuselage. Dubbed the D-2086, this aircraft was designed to conduct operations from airports equipped with a minimum of ground handling facilities.[2]

In April 1963, Delta Airlines became the launch customer for this aircraft, now designated as the DC-9, when it ordered 15 aircraft (with a further 15 on option). Following its rollout, the prototype flew for the first time on February 25, 1965. Facing stiff competition from the British Aircraft Corporation's One-Eleven (BAC-111), which had already been ordered by two domestic carriers, Douglas began an intensive testing program to certify the DC-9. This resulted in the type entering commercial service for Delta Airlines on November 29, 1965, just a little more than nine months following its first flight.[3]

The design of the DC-9 was such that it could be offered in a family of variants to fulfill a wide range of customer requirements. As such, the initial variant, the DC-9-10, was followed by a series of versions incorporating a mix of longer fuselages, wing design modifications, and more powerful engines.

Allegheny Airlines operated a large fleet of DC-9-31s, including this example which is shown in the air carrier's colors in use at the time of the crash of Flight 853. (Author's Collection)

The first DC-9-30, a variant with a fuselage stretched by 15 feet, took to the skies on August 1, 1966, and entered revenue service with Eastern Airlines the following February.[4] Measuring 119 feet 4 inches in length, the DC-9-30 model can carry 115 passengers in a five abreast seating arrangement, 25 more than the shorter DC-9-10.[5]

On August 7, 1968, the Federal Aviation Administration issued an airworthiness certificate to Allegheny Airlines for a DC-9-31 registered as N988VJ.[6] This airline was an early customer for this variant when it ordered four examples on April 28, 1965. All told, Allegheny eventually acquired sixty-one DC-9-31s.[7] Possessing excellent short field performance characteristics, and capable of terminal turnarounds as short as 23 minutes from engine shutdown to departure clearance, this aircraft fit well into Allegheny's network of short haul services.[8]

On September 9, 1969, a little over a year after entering service for Allegheny, N988VJ was operating as Flight 853 when it departed Boston, Massachusetts bound for Baltimore, Maryland. Flight 853 was a regularly scheduled flight from Boston to St. Louis, Missouri, with intermediate stops at Baltimore, Cincinnati, Ohio; and Indianapolis, Indiana.

In command of Flight 853 was 47 year-old, Captain James M. Elrod, a pilot with ratings in both single and multi-engine aircraft. At the time of the accident, Elrod had accumulated 23,813 total flying hours, 900 of which were in the DC-9. Also holding ratings for single and multi-engine aircraft, First Officer William E. Heckendorn, aged 26, had amassed 2,980 total flight hours, with 651 of these hours earned while operating the DC-9.[9]

On this particular flight, the aircraft had a gross takeoff weight of 98,589 pounds, just shy of its maximum allowable limit of 98,600 pounds.[10] The flight continued routinely to Baltimore and on to Cincinnati, where N988VJ departed at 3:15 p.m. for the short hop to the Weir County Municipal Airport, some 98 miles away.[11] Besides the two pilots, two flight attendants and seventy-eight passengers were aboard the Allegheny DC-9 as it streaked into the sky and headed towards Indianapolis.

As Allegheny 853 was departing Cincinnati, a student pilot by the name of Robert W. Carey, age 34, was preparing to takeoff from the Brookside Airpark, located approximately 20 miles northeast of Indianapolis. For this flight, Carey had leased a Piper PA-28-140 Cherokee, registration number N7374J, owned by the Forth Corporation, with the intention of making a solo cross-country flight to the Purdue University Airport as part of his quest in obtaining a private pilot's license. Prior to takeoff, however, foul weather had forced Carey to change his destination to the Bakalar Air Force Base, forty miles to the south of Brookside.[12]

The Piper PA-28-140 is a two-place trainer version of Piper's popular Cherokee all-metal general aviation aircraft. With a 30-foot wingspan, this light aircraft measures 23 feet 4 inches in length and incorporates a fixed landing gear. Since its first flight in 1960, the Cherokee has been produced in numerous variants to meet the various needs of the general aviation community.

The Forth Corporation received an airworthiness certificate for N7374J on July 26, 1968, just two weeks prior to Allegheny Airlines receiving a similar endorsement for their DC-9. Powered by its original Lycoming 0-320-E2A engine, the Piper Cherokee involved in this accident had accumulated 803 flight hours at the time of its last 100 hour inspection, which took place on August 29, 1969.[13]

Prior to departing the Brookside Airpark, Robert Carey filed a visual flight rules (VFR) flight plan specifying an intended cruising altitude of 3,500 feet. Although no one witnessed his takeoff, the airfield's general manager later testified that Carey was wearing his required eyeglasses and had turned on the Cherokee's anti-collision beacon prior to departure.[14]

Although a definite time could not be determined as to the exact moment Robert Carey departed the small airfield, he did make radio contact at 3:21 p.m. with the Indianapolis Flight Service Station. Informing the ground station of his departure from Brookside, Carey requested the activation of his flight plan. This message was to be the last received from the student pilot.

Meanwhile, the Allegheny jet was progressing quickly along its short trip between Cincinnati and Indianapolis. At 3:22 p.m., the controller at the Indianapolis Air Route Traffic Control Center (ARTCC) informed Flight 853 that he had made radar contact and issued instructions for a descent to 6,000 feet. While descending from 10,000 feet, the Allegheny DC-9 was instructed to contact Indianapolis Approach Control.

At 3:27 p.m., the approach controller made contact with the crew of the airliner, "Allegheny eight five three roger, squawk ident heading two eight zero radar vector visual approach three one left." Within a few seconds of their acknowledgement of this transmission, the crew of the DC-9 was instructed to perform a descent to 2,500 feet. A few moments later, the ground controller received what was to be the last radio message from the Allegheny jet, "Eight five three cleared down to two thousand five hundred and report reaching."[15]

Almost immediately following this last transmission, the approach controller's attention was diverted to other duties, including the radar handoff of Allegheny 820, a flight approaching from the southwest. When his attention returned to Allegheny 853, at approximately 3:31 p.m., he noticed that the aircraft had disappeared from the radar screen.

Continuing its descent to below 4,000 feet, the DC-9 passed through a layer of broken clouds. During this time, it was descending at a rate of approximately 2,460 feet per minute, which had related to an airspeed increase from 236 to 256 knots (272 to 295 mph).[16]

As the DC-9 broke through the cloud layer, Captain Elrod and First Officer Heckendorn were unaware that their aircraft was now on a collision course with Robert Carey's Piper Cherokee. A portion of the Allegheny jetliner's descent was made under VFR conditions, where the "see and avoid" concept applies.[17] The same rule applied to Robert Carey's entire flight as he made his way towards Bakalar AFB. As such, it was the responsibility of both the crew of the DC-9 and the student pilot to maintain visual scans for other air traffic. In this situation, however, the base of the clouds in relation to the operating altitude of the opposing aircraft severely restricted the effectiveness of the pilots to spot conflicting traffic.

As the Piper Cherokee continued southwards on a heading of 175 degrees, and the Allegheny jetliner sped towards Indianapolis on a course of 282 degrees, the distance between the two aircraft decreased rapidly. At 10.2 seconds before the collision, just a few moments after the DC-9 would have emerged from the cloud base, only 5,430 feet separated the two aircraft.[18]

Throughout the sequence of events leading up to this time, the Piper Cherokee had remained unobserved on two independent radar systems. At the time of the accident, the ARSR-1E serving the Indianapolis ARTCC was operating in a low-power setting to reduce atmospheric interference. While this mode of operation improved the quality of transponder information displayed on the controller's screen, it also reduced the radar's detection capabilities. Therefore, a target such as the Piper Cherokee, with its low radar cross-section, might go undetected at ranges exceeding 20 miles from the antenna site.[19] Under such conditions, ground controllers were unable to warn either the crew of the Allegheny DC-9 or the pilot of the Cherokee of a traffic conflict.

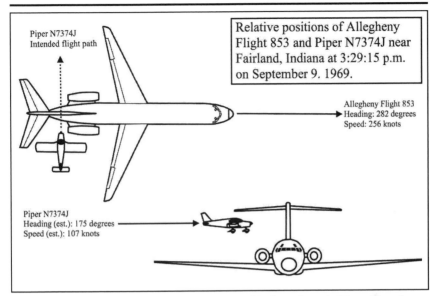

Piper N7374J
Intended flight path

Relative positions of Allegheny
Flight 853 and Piper N7374J near
Fairland, Indiana at 3:29:15 p.m.
on September 9. 1969.

Allegheny Flight 853
Heading: 282 degrees
Speed: 256 knots

Piper N7374J
Heading (est.): 175 degrees
Speed (est.): 107 knots

A diagram illustrating the relative positions of Robert Carey's Piper Cherokee
and Allegheny Flight 853 just moments before the midair collision.

It is impossible to know whether the pilots aboard either aircraft made visual contact with each other in the moments before the collision. What is certain, however, is that at 3:29 p.m. the two aircraft came together in the skies above central Indiana at an altitude of approximately 3,550 feet.

Traveling southbound, the left forward side of the Piper Cherokee struck the right side of the DC-9's tail, just below the horizontal stabilizer. The estimated closure rate between the two aircraft at the time of the collision was 504 feet per second (344 mph). The impact most likely killed Robert Carey instantly as it tore the fuselage of his small plane to pieces before it began falling to earth. The collision also separated the horizontal stabilizer from the Allegheny jetliner, causing an immediate departure from controlled flight.

As their aircraft plummeted towards the ground, Captain

Elrod and First Officer Heckendorn struggled to regain some level of control. Without its horizontal stabilizer, however, there was no chance to recover the aircraft. Approximately twelve seconds after the collision, while upside down, but with wings almost level, the Allegheny DC-9 plunged into the ground, killing all those aboard.

Narrowly missing a trailer park, and thereby averting a disaster on an even larger scale, the jetliner came down in a soybean field four miles northwest of the small community of Fairland, Indiana. Located just 250 feet away from the impact site, the crash of the doomed jet showered the Shady Acres Mobile Home Park with jet fuel, debris, and body parts.[20]

While debris from Flight 853 caused significant property damage to the nearby mobile homes, there were no injuries among the residents. There were, however, a number of narrow escapes. In one example, only three feet separated a mother and her infant daughter from life and death when an oxygen tank from the DC-9 ripped through the roof of their trailer home.[21]

Several persons in the area at the time of the accident witnessed the collision as the two aircraft came together in the sky above them. The following excerpt appeared in the *Anderson Daily Bulletin* on September 10, 1969, and is representative of most eyewitness accounts published at the time of the accident:

> A witness to the disaster, Norman W. Bennett, 23, said he looked up at the time of the collision. "The back end fell off the passenger plane, and it turned over nose-down and dropped to the ground."

Within ten minutes of the accident, police and fire department personnel began arriving at the scene. It quickly became apparent, however, that all of those aboard the two aircraft had perished. At 3:50 p.m., the National Transportation Safety Board received notification of the accident, and began the process of dispatching a team of investigators to the crash site.

The sixteen person investigative team arrived at the scene of the crash by the morning of September 10, 1969. Assisted by 500 police personnel, the federal investigators began the arduous task of searching the debris field for clues as to what had taken place.[22]

Among the many obstacles law enforcement officials confronted while securing the scene of the disaster was the presence of looters attempting to flee with valuables collected from amongst the debris. Another danger presented itself overhead in the form of private planes making passes over the area at heights as low as 300 feet.[23]

Although Investigators found the wreckage of the two aircraft scattered over an area roughly measuring 3,500 by 5,000 feet, it was concentrated in two distinct debris fields. With the exception of components torn off in the midair collision, the wreckage of DC-9 indicated that it was generally intact when it hit the ground. The impact site of this aircraft measured approximately 1,300 feet in length and 700 feet in width.[24]

The wreckage of the Piper Cherokee and the horizontal stabilizer of the DC-9 were located some 4,500 feet to the east of the primary crash site. A large portion of the single engine aircraft's fuselage, along with its left wing and horizontal stabilizers, were found to be lying intact approximately 150 feet east of the Allegheny jet's horizontal stabilizer. The light plane's

131

engine, propeller, vertical fin, and the majority of its remaining wreckage was found 700 feet south of the DC-9's horizontal stabilizer.[25] The wreckage of both aircraft was transported to Bakalar Air Force Base, near Columbus, Indiana, where a partial reconstruction was performed to determine the actual impact geometry between the aircraft.

Both the flight data and cockpit voice recorders from Allegheny 853 were recovered from the crash site. Investigators found the casing of the flight data recorder had been severely deformed by the accident. After technicians cut the recorder open, it was found that the foil tape inside was torn in half at the point of the last recorded traces. Nonetheless, investigators were able to reconstruct this recording and obtain a reading on the traces. These indicated that the Allegheny jet was flying at 256 knots on a heading of 282 degrees and descending at approximately 2,400 feet a minute at the moment of the collision. The airspeed recording stopped 13 minutes and 18 seconds after the aircraft had taken off from Cincinnati. One second later, the remaining parameter traces became erratic, the last altitude trace prior to the onset of these abnormalities being 3,550 feet.[26]

Upon reviewing the cockpit voice recorder, investigators found that the DC-9's crew was operating their aircraft within normal parameters in preparation for landing. This recorder unit was also heavily damaged in the crash, its tape cartridge becoming exposed. Despite this, the tape recording survived intact and provided useful data. Detailing the last few seconds of Flight 853, the following is an excerpt taken from the transcript created from this recording by the NTSB:

> 1529:13   [F/O] Out of thirty-five for twenty-five.
> 1529:14.3 [CAPT] I'm going down.
> 1529:15   [*Sound similar to objects striking metal.*]
>   [*Landing gear warning horn.*]

1529:17   [*Sound of possible stall vibration.*]
1529:27.1 [*Recording ends.*]

The Captain's statement made at 1529:14.3 is somewhat provocative in that it could indicate that he spotted the onrushing Cherokee just moments before the collision and was attempting to dive under it. In fact, he did not finish this remark until nearly one second after the sound of the collision occurred at 1529:15. The more likely explanation, however, is that he was merely acknowledging the descent as called out by the First Officer.

The investigation into this accident revealed the complex nature of operating low and high speed aircraft within a terminal area under both passive and active control. In this instance, such a practice was complicated further by the prevailing weather conditions. Although specific data was unavailable, investigators estimated that a layer of broken clouds, with a base of 4,000 feet, existed in the area at the time of the accident. By using this parameter, it was determined that only 14 seconds elapsed between the time that the Allegheny DC-9 descended below the cloud layer and the collision. These fourteen seconds represent the only time available to the pilots of both aircraft to spot each other and initiate evasive action.[27]

Although within regulations, the NTSB considered descent rate of Flight 853 (2,500 feet/min) to be somewhat high in the context of existing regulations permitting visual flight rules operations only 500 feet below the cloud layer in airport approach areas.[28]

On July 15, 1970, the National Transportation Safety board published the findings of its investigation into the collision between Allegheny Flight 853 and N7374J. In this report, the investigators determined the following as the probable cause of this air disaster:

> The Board determines the probable cause of this accident to be the deficiencies in the collision avoidance capability of the Air Traffic Control (ATC) system of the Federal Aviation Administration in a terminal area wherein there was mixed Instrument Flight Rules (IFR) and Visual Flight Rules (VFR) traffic. The deficiencies included the inadequacy of the see-and-avoid concept under the circumstances of this case; the technical limitations of radar in detecting all aircraft; and the absence of Federal Aviation Regulations which would provide a system of adequate separation of mixed VFR and IFR traffic in terminal areas.

As of 2013, the 83 people killed on September 9, 1969 in the midair collision of Allegheny 853 and N7374J still represents the highest death toll of any aviation accident in Indiana's history. Among those killed in this disaster from this state was James M. Elrod, captain of the Allegheny DC-9, and Robert Carey, pilot of the Piper Cherokee. The dead from the Hoosier state also included Jerry Kulinski, manager and co-owner of Radio Station WVTS of West Terra Haute, Dr. Robert H. Kohr, a mechanical engineering professor at Purdue University, and Mrs. Morris Groverman, wife of the southern division manager of the Northern Indiana Public Service Co. of Monticello.[29]

A relatively new design at the time of this crash, the McDonnell Douglas DC-9 went on to become one of the best selling passenger aircraft in the world. Built in five major variants for airlines around the globe, production of the DC-9 ended in 1982.[30] Prior to this, however, McDonnell Douglas had introduced a heavily redesigned version that was designated first as the DC-9 Super 80, and later as the MD-80.

To serve a broad range of customers, the MD-80, like its predecessor, was produced in a wide array of variants. In 1989, McDonald Douglas introduced the MD-90, which incorporated International Aero Engines (IAE) V2500 turbofans in place of the Pratt & Whitney JT8D engines, versions of which had powered every DC-9 and MD-80 aircraft built up to that time.[31]

Following Boeing's acquisition of McDonnell Douglas in August 1997, the decision was made to halt production of the MD-90 in 2000. In 1994, McDonnell Douglas began work on the MD-95, which Boeing later redesignated as the 717. Although Boeing enjoyed some success in marketing the 717, it eventually ceased producing the aircraft in 2005 in favor of concentrating on its family of 737 jetliners.

Nearly seventeen years after the crash of Flight 853, an eerily similar event occurred in the crowded skies over southern California. On August 31, 1986, an Aeromexico DC-9-32, operating as Flight 498, was on approach to the Los Angeles International Airport (LAX) when it was involved in a mid-air collision with a Piper Cherokee over the city of Cerritos, California at an altitude of 6,560 feet.[32]

In an almost exact repeat of the 1969 disaster in Indiana, the DC-9 lost its horizontal stabilizer and part of its tail in the collision with the light plane. The three persons aboard the Cherokee were killed instantly. Meanwhile, the Aeromexico DC-9 began its final descent to earth as it spiraled out of control. A few seconds later, the jetliner crashed in a huge fireball, killing all 64 aboard along with 15 others on the ground.

Nearly all aircraft accidents have resulted in improving the safety of air travel, and the crashes of Allegheny 853 and

135

Aeromexico 498 were no exception. Accidents such as these have driven the development of new regulations and improved safety technology such as the Traffic Alert and Collision Avoidance System (TCAS), both of which have significantly reduced the frequency of midair collisions.

Chapter Thirteen
Fatal Flaw

On the morning of January 28, 1970, seven passengers began arriving at Cleveland, Ohio's Burke Lakefront Airport, where they were to board a de Havilland DH.104 Dove operated by TAG Airlines.[1] As its name implies, this airfield is located on the shores of Lake Erie, the shallowest of the five Great Lakes. On this particular morning, those boarding the small commuter plane had purchased tickets for the air carrier's 7:30 a.m. flight to Detroit, Michigan.[2] After the passengers were secured in the cabin, the aircraft's two pilots, seated at the controls in their elevated cockpit, began taxiing the DH.104 towards the small airport's single runway. Unseen through the prevailing overcast, that morning's sunrise was just beginning to brighten the gray skies above one of the largest cities in the state of Ohio. Departing the airport as scheduled, the twin-engine airliner began climbing over the ice-covered waters of Lake Erie as it embarked upon a journey it was destined never to complete.

As was the case with the Vickers Viscount, described separately in this book, the design of the de Havilland DH.104 Dove resulted from a specification issued by Great Britain's Brabazon Committee. Established during the later years of World War II, this organization was tasked with determining the requirements of that nation's postwar civil airliner market.

On September 25, 1945, the de Havilland DH.104 flew for the first time, thus becoming the first civil transport to fly in Britain following the end of Second World War.[3] Filling the requirement for a small commuter airliner and executive aircraft, the Dove appeared in a number of variants during its production history. Finding service with both civil and military operators, 542 DH.104 Doves were built before production ended during the mid-1960s.

Among the smaller air carriers that acquired the DH.104 for their operational requirements was TAG Airlines. Founded in 1955, and based at the Detroit City Airport, this small airline focused upon executive travel between major cities in the Great Lakes region. On December 5, 1963, TAG placed a newly acquired DH.104 Dove into service on its network of short distance, high frequency routes. Built in Britain during 1953, this aircraft was originally registered as G-ANFD, prior to its subsequent sale to an American operator later that year. Following this transaction, the twin-engine airliner was registered in the United States as N1588V. This registration was retained until its sale to TAG Airlines, after which it was changed to N2300H.

Unlike the major air carriers that operated mostly out of airports bordering large metropolitan areas, TAG Airlines provided service between smaller airfields located nearer to a city's downtown area. In addition to Cleveland, other cities served by TAG from its base of operations at Detroit during the 1950s and 1960s included Akron and Chicago. For a brief time during the late 1950s, the commuter airline also offered service to Rockford, Illinois. Catering to business people, brochures printed by TAG Airlines throughout its history emphasized the time saving benefits of flying aboard its aircraft compared to

Tag Airlines —THE QUICKEST WAY!

Because its planes land at downtown airports, TAG has won wide endorsement in the business communities of Cleveland and Detroit. No other form of public transportation can save you so much time. These examples illustrate how TAG CUTS TRAVEL TIME:

TAG INVITES YOU TO CHECK THESE COMPARISONS!	DOWNTOWN AREAS BETWEEN	TAG AIRLINES	OTHER TYPICAL AIRLINES, IN- CLUDING LIMOU- SINE FROM DOWN- TOWN TO AIRPORT	AVERAGE TIME SAVED		Cabs and Rent-A-Car Service are available at all airports.
				ONE WAY	ROUND TRIP	
	CLEVELAND - DETROIT	45 min.	2 hrs. 53 min.	2 hrs. 8 min.	4 hrs. 16 min.	

An advertisement issued by TAG Airlines highlighting the time saving benefits of the carrier's routes compared to its competitors. (Author's Collection)

those operated by the major airlines out of airports located on a city's outskirts.

By the morning of January 20, 1970, N2300H had provided just over six years of dependable service to TAG Airlines. Operating as Flight 730, this aircraft was scheduled to fly a route over which it had undoubtedly traversed on numerous occasions since being placed into operation within TAG's narrow scope of destinations.

In command of N2300H for this flight was Captain Jake Feldman. Born on October 20, 1925, the 44-year-old pilot had been employed by TAG since May of 1965. Feldman had previously worked for a number of air carriers, including Boone County Aviation, Capital Airways, and Zantop. During his flying career, Captain Feldman had logged 2,000 of his 10,200 flight hours aboard DH.104 aircraft. During a proficiency check conducted by a company check pilot on November 26, 1969, Captain Feldman also received a route certification.

Seated next to Captain Feldman in the two-person cockpit was First Officer Robert G. Arthur. Having previously worked for Beaver Aviation of Beaver Falls, Pennsylvania, the 26-year-old pilot had been with TAG Airlines since April 1969. By the time Flight 730 departed Cleveland on the morning of January 28, 1970, Robert Arthur had amassed nearly half of his 1,475 hours of flight experience operating de Havilland DH.104 type aircraft.[4]

Cleared for takeoff at 7:37 a.m. by the Burke Lakefront Airport control tower, the crew of Flight 730 advanced power on the aircraft's two 400 horsepower Gipsy Queen 70 Mk 2 engines. Responding almost immediately, the twin piston engines began pushing the 8,600-pound aircraft down the runway. A few seconds later, after performing an entirely normal takeoff, the TAG airliner rose into the sky.

Becoming airborne, the crew of the small airliner raised its landing gear even as it gained altitude in the gray overcast sky. Leaving Cleveland behind, the commuter plane began following a course that would take it over Lake Erie and southern Ontario as it made its way to Detroit, some 92 miles, or approximately 45 minutes flying time, away.

Eight minutes after taking off, the crew of Flight 730 was instructed to contact Cleveland Center, an air traffic control facility that would guide the airliner until it neared the Detroit City Airport. A few moments later, at 7:45 a.m., First Officer Arthur established communication with Cleveland Center, during which he reported the TAG airliner reaching its 4,000-foot clearance altitude. After establishing radar contact, the controller at the busy air traffic control facility radioed the current altimeter setting for Detroit. In what was to become the final radio transmission received from the ill-fated plane, the first officer made a routine acknowledgment of the altimeter setting. The time was 7:46 a.m., and the routine nature of Flight 730's trek across Lake Erie was only minutes away from taking a tragic turn.

At 7:49, just three minutes after receiving the last communication from the TAG airliner, the controller at Cleveland Center noticed that Flight 730 was no longer appearing on his radarscope. After noticing this discrepancy, and with the hope that the aircraft had suffered a transponder problem, the controller made repeated, but ultimately unsuccessful, attempts to contact the missing aircraft. The disappearance of the commuter plane was also noticed by personnel operating the radar system at the Selfridge Air Force Base, near Mount Clemens, Michigan.[5]

Apprised of the situation, search teams began scouring the ice-covered lake for any sign of the missing commuter plane. This search quickly yielded results as a hole in the ice, surrounded by aircraft debris, was discovered just before 9:30 that morning. A survey of the available wreckage confirmed that it belonged to the TAG airliner. The site of the crash was fixed as being approximately 22 miles northwest of the Burke Lakefront Airport, or 14 miles due north of Avon Lake, Ohio. Unable to locate any signs of survivors, search teams quickly lost hope that any of the nine persons aboard the aircraft had survived its final plunge.

One of the lead agencies conducting the search for Flight 730 was the United States Coast Guard (USCG). Among the assets committed to the search were two helicopters, a 44-foot search and rescue boat, and the cutters *Bramble* and *Kaw*.[6] Considering the time of year during which this accident occurred, the early search operation benefited from generally good weather conditions. The Great Lakes, however, are notorious for their rapidly changing weather conditions. Therefore, it comes as little surprise that within twenty-four hours of the crash the U.S. Weather Bureau had issued gale warnings for Lake Erie.

Searchers arriving at the wreck site found that the majority of the airliner had broken through the 12 to 14 inches of ice covering that section of Lake Erie. Two major holes, spaced about sixty feet apart, were discovered in the ice. The largest of

A pair of de Havilland DH.104 Doves operated by TAG Airlines at the Burke Lakefront Airport, near downtown Cleveland. (Author's Collection)

these was approximately 120 feet in diameter, and was presumably where the primary section of the aircraft impacted before sinking to the bottom of the lake in 80 feet of water. The smaller hole, which was within a series of cracks radiating from the principal impact cavity, measured around 40 feet wide. Scattered on the surface ice around these impact sites was a small amount of debris, consisting primarily of the aircraft's structure. While some diving operations to explore the wreckage were conducted shortly after the crash, a concentrated effort to recover this debris had to await the onset of better weather later that year.

Informed of the crash, the National Transportation Safety Board (NTSB) dispatched an investigative team, which arrived at the Burke Lakefront Airport late in the afternoon on the day of the accident. Although most of the TAG airliner's wreckage was resting on the bottom of the lake, it was readily apparent early in the investigation that an in-flight structural failure had occurred.

During the initial recovery operation, nearly 90 percent of the aircraft's left wing and a 15-foot section of its outer right wing were retrieved from the surface of the ice. The outer section of the right wing exhibited a jagged edge along the line at which it separated from the airliner. This evidence supported an early theory that the crash of Flight 730 was caused when a failure in the right engine's mounting framework allowed that powerplant, with its attached propeller still turning, to pivot around its outboard mount. In such an event, the arc of the propeller would have crossed the wing's outer section, severing it from the aircraft.

Examining the outer section of the right wing, investigators found a series of paint smears on its surface and deicing strip. Also discovered was a black residue adhering to the deicer strip. A subsequent analysis confirmed that the paint samples taken from the wing section were identical to the paint used on the aircraft's engine nacelles. Meanwhile, the black residue found on the wing deicer boot was determined as having come from the rubber deicing boots installed on the shanks of the propeller blades.

A priority for recovery forces was to retrieve the remains of the aircraft's crew and passengers. Throughout the recovery operation, the bodies of both pilots and five of the seven passengers were brought to the surface. The two passengers not located in the wreckage, were officially listed as missing by the NTSB in its final report concerning the crash of Flight 730.[7]

On March 29, 1970, barely two months after the accident, the NTSB released a preliminary report concerning the crash of Flight 730. This narrative supported the theory that an in-flight separation of the right engine had caused the commuter plane to crash by cutting off a section of its right wing.[8]

With the vast majority of the crashed airliner lying some eighty feet below the surface of Lake Erie, however, it was imperative that this wreckage be recovered. When completed, the entire salvage operation succeeded in recovering nearly 98 percent of N2300H's wreckage. Following recovery, the wreckage was transported to a warehouse, where a detailed examination could be conducted.[9]

The right engine of the de Havilland Dove was found on the lake floor nearly 75 feet away from the primary wreckage field. Sifting through the murky bottom of the lake, recovery forces found no structural components near the location at which the right engine was discovered. With the exception of one blade, the entire propeller assembly was still attached to this engine. Overall, the damage to the propeller assembly was nearly identical to that sustained by the corresponding assembly attached to the left engine. Upon being brought to the surface, the entire mounting framework associated with the right engine was found still attached to the inboard section of the right wing.

As the investigation continued, the evidence revealed by the newly recovered wreckage indicated that an in-flight structural failure had not occurred in the right engine's attachment framework. The nearly identical bending of both the inboard and outboard mounting frames for the right engine revealed that they had not failed until the engine had pivoted nearly 90 degrees to the right. Furthermore, had the engine attachment failed, it could be expected that these components would have separated from the aircraft along with the engine.

On the final day of scheduled recovery operations, investigators were presented with the key to unlock the mystery when the right wing's lower root joint attach fitting was brought to the surface. An examination of this critical component revealed that it had failed in flight. Carrying the entire load of weight and lift transmitted from the fuselage to the wing, the failure of this component aboard the TAG airliner resulted in its right wing folding upwards alongside the fuselage.[10]

As the commuter plane plummeted out of control during its final descent from 4,000 feet, the forces involved caused the right engine to separate from its mountings. Passing across the bottom of the wing, the propeller cut through the structure of the outer wing section, thus causing a complete wing failure.

In 1961, some nine years before this accident, the aircraft's manufacturer became aware that a chromium plating process performed upon the lower root joint attach fitting effectively reduced the lifespan of this component to 10,000 flying hours. As a result, a recommendation was issued calling for the replacement of any fittings with chromium plating during the next removal of an affected aircraft's wings or prior to 10,000 flying hours. Although this requirement became compulsory for aircraft registered in the United Kingdom, it did not become mandatory in the United States. Instead, the Federal Aviation Administration (FAA) issued Airworthiness Directive (AD) 61-18 -3, which reiterated the requirement to replace any chromium-plated fittings prior to the accumulation of 10,000 flight hours, but omitted the recommendation to replace such components during the next wing removal.[11]

A review of N2300H's maintenance history revealed that a wing removal was performed in November of 1965. As part of this overhaul, new pins were installed in the aircraft, which maintenance personnel mistakenly interpreted as complying with the FAA's AD 61-18-3. While the persons involved in this work stated they knew of the requirement to replace the chromium-plated fittings prior to the accumulation of 10,000 flight hours, they could provide no explanation as to why new pins were installed.[12]

Investigators found fault with the FAA's adoption of a more lenient approach to addressing the chromium-plated fitting problem than was recommended by the aircraft's manufacturer. Had the requirement to replace all such fittings during the next wing removal not been omitted by the FAA, it is reasonable to assume that the failure of the wing fitting, and therefore the crash, would have been prevented.

Nearly one year following the crash of Flight 730, the NTSB released a report detailing the particulars of the disaster. In contrast to a number of other crashes, no fault could be placed on the pilots or operator of the downed aircraft. In the report, however, some responsibility for the accident was directed at the FAA, as related in the following excerpt:

> The Board determines that the probable cause of this accident was the in-flight failure of the lower, right, main wing-to-fuselage root joint attach fitting resulting from undetected fatigue cracks in the wing portion of the fitting. The Board also finds that the Federal Aviation Administration's requirement for the timely replacement of chromium-plated root joint fittings was inadequate.

The loss of N2300H represented the first crash of an aircraft belonging to TAG Airlines. At the time of the accident, it was widely reported in the press that the airline was in the process of expanding its operations.[13] These plans would never materialize, however, as the airline ceased operations shortly following the crash of Flight 730.

One year after the TAG airliner crashed into icy Lake Erie, an eerily similar accident occurred in the skies over the American Southwest. On May 6, 1971, a de Havilland Dove (N4922V) lost its right wing and crashed near Coolidge, Arizona during a flight from Tucson to Phoenix. As was the case with Flight 730, this accident, which killed twelve, was also caused by the failure of the lower main root joint fitting.[14]

Today, with only a few examples remaining in existence around the world, the de Havilland DH.104 Dove has all but disappeared from the skies.

NOTES

Chapter One
Crash of the first "Tin Goose"

1.   This organization was also known as the Ford Air Freight Lines.
2.   Kenneth Munson. *U.S. Commercial Aircraft*, p. 19.
3.   Edward J. Vinarcik. *Ford's Tri-Motor*, Advanced Materials & Processes, October 2003, p. 51.
4.   William T. Larkins. *The Ford Tri-Motor*, p. 18.
5.   Kenneth Munson. *U.S. Commercial Aircraft*, p. 32-33.
6.   Ibid., p. 32.
7.   In 1934, this organization became the Bureau of Air Commerce.
8.   William T. Larkins. *The Ford Tri-Motor*, p. 184.
9.   The Evening Independent, May 12, 1928.
10. The Lowell Sun, May 12, 1928.
11. The Evening Independent, May 12, 1928.
12. Bill Holder & Scott Vadnais. *The "C" Planes*, p. 7.

Chapter Two
Rushed into Service

1.   Jim Winchester, *Civil Aircraft*, p. 189
2.   Kenneth Munson. *U.S. Commercial Aircraft*, p. 67.
3.   Jim Winchester, *Civil Aircraft*, p. 189.
4.   All times in this chapter are expressed in Central Standard Time (CST).
5.   Bureau of Air Commerce. *Statement of Probable Cause Concerning an Aircraft Accident Which Occurred to a Plane of Northwest Airlines on August 7, 1934 at Milwaukee, Wisconsin*, p. 1.
6.   Contemporary newspaper accounts list a wide array of spellings for the names of the individuals involved in this crash, a common occurrence when such accidents take place.
7.   A wobble pump is an auxiliary hand pump for supplying fuel to an aircraft's engine in the event of a fuel system failure.

8.   Jefferson City Post-Tribune, August 8, 1934.

9.   Ibid.

10. Bureau of Air Commerce. *Statement of Probable Cause Concerning an Aircraft Accident Which Occurred to a Plane of Northwest Airlines on August 7, 1934 at Milwaukee, Wisconsin*, p. 2.

11. Lockheed Martin. *Model 10 Electra Factsheet*.

Chapter Three
"Quite a jolt..."

1.   DC is an acronym denoting Douglas-Commercial.

2.   Len Cacutt. *The World's Greatest Aircraft*, p. 40.

3.   Wisconsin State Journal, August 8, 1949.

4.   Unless noted otherwise, all times in this chapter are expressed as Eastern Standard Time (EST).

5.   Civil Aeronautics Board. *Accident Investigation Report, Capital Airlines, Inc. and Cessna 140 – Milwaukee, Wisconsin, August 7, 1949*, p.1.

6.   Some references refer to this airfield as Maitland Airport.

7.   Civil Aeronautics Board. *Accident Investigation Report, Capital Airlines, Inc. and Cessna 140 – Milwaukee, Wisconsin, August 7, 1949*, p. 2-5.

8.   Ibid., p. 2-3.

9.   The Capital Times, August 8, 1949.

10. Civil Aeronautics Board. *Accident Investigation Report, Capital Airlines, Inc. and Cessna 140 – Milwaukee, Wisconsin, August 7, 1949*, p. 3.

11. Not to be confused with another DC-3 operated by this company, registered as N28PR (MSN 6323), which crashed on March 1, 1989.

Chapter Four
A Troubled Design

1.   William Green, Gordon Swanborough, John Mowinski. *Modern Commercial Airliners*, p. 144.

2.   Kenneth Munson. *Airliners from 1919 to the Present Day*, p. 278.

3. During this timeframe, Northwest Airlines also operated as Northwest Orient.

4. Unless otherwise noted, all of the times in this chapter are expressed in Central Standard Time (CST).

5. Civil Aeronautics Board. *Accident Investigation Report, Northwest Airlines, Inc., Almelund, Minnesota, October 13, 1950*, p. 1.

6. The Winona Republican-Herald, October 13, 1950.

7. Lubbock Morning Avalanche, October 14, 1950.

8. Civil Aeronautics Board. *Accident Investigation Report, Northwest Airlines, Inc., Almelund, Minnesota, October 13, 1950*, p. 1.

9. The phenolic resin had been applied to the valve at the time of manufacture.

10. Civil Aeronautics Board. *Accident Investigation Report, Northwest Airlines, Inc., Almelund, Minnesota, October 13, 1950*, p. 4.

11. Winona Republican-Herald, April 23, 1951.

12. Geza Szurovy. *Classic American Airlines*, p. 132.

13. Kenneth Munson. *U.S. Commercial Aircraft*, p. 121.

Chapter Five
The Danger of Ice

1. During the 1960s, the O'Hare International Airport became the world's busiest airport. As of 2011, it was ranked fourth among the busiest airports around the globe.

2. Marcelle Size Knaack. *Encyclopedia of U.S. Air Force Aircraft and Missile Systems, Volume II, Post-World War II Bombers 1945-1973*, p. 466.

3. The U.S. Army Air Corps became the U.S. Army Air Forces in June 1941.

4. Marcelle Size Knaack. *Encyclopedia of U.S. Air Force Aircraft and Missile Systems, Volume II, Post-World War II Bombers 1945-1973*, p. 471.

5. U.S. Air Force Fact Sheet. *Douglas B-26C in Air National Guard Service*.

6. Some early aircraft were equipped various combinations of .50 caliber machine guns and 37mm or 75mm cannons.

7. U.S. Air Force Fact Sheet. *Douglas A-26C*.

8. The Laredo Times, January 15, 1951.

9. The La Crosse Tribune, January 15, 1951.

10. Clovis News-Journal. January 15, 1951.

11. Traverse City Record-Eagle, January 15, 1951.

12. Ibid.

Chapter Six
...a "marvelous job" of crash-landing...

1. All time in this chapter is expressed as Eastern Standard Time (EST).

2. William Green, Gordon Swanborough, John Mowinski. *Modern Commercial Aircraft*, p. 100.

3. Kenneth Munson. *Airliners From 1919 to the Present Day*, p. 279.

4. Simply stated, brake mean effective pressure (BMEP) is a measurement used to determine the useful output of a reciprocating engine.

5. The Racine Journal-Times, January 21, 1954.

6. Civil Aeronautics Board. *Accident Investigation Board, Aircraft Investigation Report, American Airlines, Inc., Near Buffalo, New York, on January 20, 1954*, p. 4.

7. Ibid., p. 3.

8. Kenneth Munson. *U.S. Civil Airliners*, p. 119.

9. Ibid., p. 168.

Chapter Seven
"...a descent at too high an airspeed..."

1. Len Cacutt. *The World's Greatest Aircraft*, p. 126.

2. Ibid., p. 127.

3. Air Canada. *Historical Fleet Information: Vickers Viscount.*

4. Unless noted otherwise, all times in this chapter are related as Eastern Standard Time (EST).

5. The Hammond Times, July 10, 1956.

6. Civil Aeronautics Board. *Accident Investigation Report, Trans-Canada Air Lines Viscount, CF-TGR, Flat Rock, Michigan, July 9, 1956,* Supplement Data.

7. Ibid., p. 2.

8. Ibid., p. 4.

9. Air Canada operated the Viscount until 1974.

10. William Green, Gordon Swanborough, & John Mowinski. *Modern Commercial Aircraft,* p. 168.

Chapter Eight
"Pull it up!"

1. Stewart Wilson. *Douglas DC-6/7,* p. 37.

2. Bill Yenne. *The Story of the Boeing Company,* p. 142.

3. Stewart Wilson. *Douglas DC-6/7,* p. 26.

4. Ibid., p. 61.

5. Unless noted otherwise, all times in this chapter are expressed in Central Daylight Time (CDT).

6. The air carrier was also known as Northwest Orient during this phase of its history.

7. Civil Aeronautics Board. A*ircraft Accident Report, Northwest Airlines, Inc., Douglas DC-6B, N 575, Minneapolis, Minnesota, August 28, 1958,* p. 2. A transmissometer consists of a light projector and a receiver. Light projected at a fixed intensity reaches the receiver either as projected or diminished in proportion to the level of visibility reducing particles in the atmosphere such as smoke and fog.

8. Austin Daily Herald, August 28, 1958.

9. Civil Aeronautics Board. A*ircraft Accident Report, Northwest Airlines, Inc., Douglas DC-6B, N 575, Minneapolis, Minnesota, August 28, 1958,* p. 7.

10. The Daily Republic. August 28, 1958.

11. Civil Aeronautics Board. A*ircraft Accident Report, Northwest Airlines, Inc., Douglas DC-6B, N 575, Minneapolis, Minnesota, August 28, 1958,* p. 9-10.

12. Ibid., p. 10-11.

13. Stewart Wilson. *Douglas DC-6/7*, p. 34.

14. Kenneth Munson. *U.S. Commercial Aircraft*, p. 126.

Chapter Nine
A Tale of Two British Bombers

1. William Green. *The World's Fighting Planes*, p. 120.

2. John W. R. Taylor & Gordon Swanborough. *Military Aircraft of the World*, p. 73.

3. William Green. *The World's Fighting Planes*, p. 120.

4. Some sources indicate the Vulcan's destination as Offutt AFB, Nebraska. Contemporary accounts published in Britain at the time of the accident name Lincoln AFB as the aircraft's intended destination.

5. Flight and Aircraft Engineer, October 31, 1958. *Loss of Vulcan in U.S.A.*, p. 680.

6. Hamilton Journal, October 29, 1958.

7. The Lowell Sun, October 25, 1958.

8. Traverse City Record-Eagle, October 27, 1958.

9. The Holland Evening Sentinel, November 13, 1958.

10. The Ludington Daily News, June 20, 1959.

11. Avro was a division of British aircraft manufacturer Hawker Siddeley before being merged with its owning company in 1963.

12. William Green. *The World's Fighting Planes*, p. 121-122.

13. The Odessa American, August 13, 1978.

14. The Chronicle-Telegram, August 12, 1978.

15. Ibid.

Chapter Ten
"No...No!!"

1. As of 2013, Chicago is the third largest city in the United States, following New York and Los Angeles.

2. Some sources use the T&WA acronym to describe this airline at this stage in its history. Literature produced by the airline during this timeframe, however, employs the TWA acronym.

3. Kenneth Munson. *U.S. Commercial Aircraft*, p. 105.

4. Ibid., p. 105.

5. Len Cacutt. *The World's Greatest Aircraft*, p. 119.

6. All times in this chapter are expressed as Central Standard Time (CST).

7. Civil Aeronautics Board. *Aircraft Accident Report, Trans World Airlines, Inc., Lockheed Constellation L-1049H, N102R, Midway Airport, Chicago, Illinois, November 24, 1959*, p. 2.

8. Ibid., p. 2.

9. The Hutchinson News, November 26, 1959.

10. The Salt Lake Tribune, November 25, 1959.

11. Salt Lake Tribune. November 25, 1959.

12. Civil Aeronautics Board. *Aircraft Accident Report, Trans World Airlines, Inc., Lockheed Constellation L-1049H, N102R, Midway Airport, Chicago, Illinois, November 24, 1959*, p. 2-5.

13. Ibid., p. 3.

14. The Sheboygan Press, November 24, 1959.

15. The Salt Lake Tribune, November 25, 1959.

16. Reported as Delean Nichols in some news stories printed at the time of the accident.

17. The Sheboygan Press, November 24, 1959.

18. San Antonio Express, November 25, 1959.

19. The Salt Lake Tribune, November 25, 1959.

20. Kingsport News, November 26, 1959.

21. The Progress, November 24, 1959.

22. The Hutchinson News, November 26, 1959.

23. Civil Aeronautics Board. *Aircraft Accident Report, Trans World Airlines, Inc., Lockheed Constellation L-1049H, N102R, Midway Airport, Chicago, Illinois, November 24, 1959*, p. 4.

24. Logansport Pharos Tribune, March 16, 1959.

25. Chicago Department of Aviation. *Monthly Operations, Passengers, Cargo Summary by Class, For December 2012, Midway Airport*, p.1.

26. Len Cacutt. *The World's Greatest Aircraft*, p. 122.

27. Kenneth Munson. *U.S. Commercial Aircraft*, p. 135.

Chapter Eleven
"There was a sudden orange flash..."

1. William Green, Gordon Swanborough, & John Mowinski. *Modern Commercial Aircraft*, p. 70.

2. Len Cacutt. *The World's Greatest Aircraft*, p. 201.

3. Boeing Commercial Airplane Company. *727 Airplane Characteristics, Airport Planning, April 1985*, p. 12&15.

4. Len Cacutt. *The World's Greatest Aircraft*, p. 201-204.

5. The 727-22 designation denotes a 727-100 manufactured for United Airlines (22).

6. Unless otherwise noted, all times in this chapters are expressed in Central Daylight Time (CDT).

7. Winnipeg Free Press, August 17, 1965.

8. Ames Daily Tribune, August 17, 1965.

9. Humboldt Standard, August 17, 1965.

10. Scottsdale Daily Progress, August 18, 1965.

11. The Daily News, August 17, 1965.

12. Humboldt Standard, August 17, 1965.

13. Amarillo Globe-Times, August 17, 1965. Note: Some published reports indicate that a temporary morgue was also established at the Great Lakes Naval Training Center.

14. The Cedar Rapids Gazette, August 17, 1965.

15. Scottsdale Daily Progress, August 18, 1965.

16. National Transportation Safety Board. *Aircraft Accident Report, United Air Lines, Inc., B-727, N7036U, In Lake Michigan, August 16, 1965*, p. 12-13.

17. Ibid., p. 11.

18. The Air Defense Command considered the second reading to be accurate within the limits of +500 or -1,000 feet (1,000-2,500 above sea level).

19. U.S. Naval Research Laboratory. *An Experimental Evaluation of Four Types of Altimeters Using Both Pilots and Enlisted Men Subjects*, p. 7.
20. The crash investigation responsibilities of the Civil Aeronautics Board were assumed by the newly formed National Transportation Safety Board on April 1, 1967.
21. Len Cacutt. *The World's Greatest Aircraft*, p. 206.
22. With over 7,000 examples built, the Boeing 737 holds the current record of the most popular jetliner ever produced.

Chapter Twelve
See and Avoid

1. Douglas Aircraft merged with the McDonnell Aircraft Corporation in 1967, becoming McDonnell Douglas.
2. Paul Eden. *Civil Aircraft Today*, p. 128-129.
3. John W. R. Taylor & Gordon Swanborough. *Civil Aircraft of the World*, p. 46.
4. Ibid., p. 47.
5. Douglas Aircraft Company. *Airplane Characteristics for Airport Planning, June 1984.*
6. National Transportation Safety Board. *Aircraft Accident Report, AAR-70-15*, Appendix C.
7. Paul Eden. *Civil Aircraft Today*, p. 133.
8. Turnaround time data obtained from page 97 of *DC-9 Airplane Characteristics for Airport Planning-June 1964*, issued by the Douglas Aircraft Company.
9. National Transportation Safety Board. *Aircraft Accident Report, AAR-70-15*, Appendix B.
10. Ibid., Appendix C.
11. All times noted in this chapter are expressed as Eastern Daylight Time (EDT).
12. Bakalar Air Force Base was deactivated in 1970. It survives today as Columbus Municipal Airport.

13. National Transportation Safety Board. *Aircraft Accident Report, AAR-70-15*, Appendix C.
14. Ibid., p. 3.
15. Ibid., p. 3.
16. Ibid., p. 10.
17. Also expressed as "see and be seen."
18. National Transportation Safety Board. *Aircraft Accident Report, AAR-70-15*, Attachment A.
19. Ibid., p. 13-14.
20. The Anderson Herald, September 10, 1969.
21. Anderson Daily Bulletin, September 10, 1969.
22. Ibid.
23. The Anderson Herald, September 10, 1969.
24. National Transportation Safety Board. *Aircraft Accident Report, AAR-70-15*, p. 7.
25. Ibid., p. 7-8.
26. Ibid., p. 6.
27. Ibid., p. 9-10.
28. Ibid., p. 16.
29. Tipton Daily Tribune, September 10, 1969.
30. McDonnell Douglas also developed the C-9 variant for the U.S. military.
31. Paul Eden. *Civil Aircraft Today*, p. 70.
32. National Transportation Safety Board. *Aircraft Accident Report, AAR-87-07*.

Chapter Thirteen
Fatal Flaw

1. Some references, including the official accident report issued by the NTSB use the DH-104 designation to identify this aircraft model. Another variation in some sources is D.H. 104.
2. All times in this chapter are expressed as Eastern Standard Time (EST).
3. John W. R. Taylor & Gordon Swanborough. *Civil Aircraft of the World*, p. 90.

4. National Transportation Safety Board. *Aircraft Accident Report, TAG Airlines, Inc., de Havilland Dove [DH-104], N2300H in Lake Erie, January 28, 1970*, Appendix B.

5. The Holland Evening Sentinel, January 28, 1970.

6. Ibid.

7. National Transportation Safety Board. *Aircraft Accident Report, TAG Airlines, Inc., de Havilland Dove [DH-104], N2300H in Lake Erie, January 28, 1970*, p. 2.

8. The Times-Reporter, March 30, 1970.

9. National Transportation Safety Board. *Aircraft Accident Report, TAG Airlines, Inc., de Havilland Dove [DH-104], N2300H in Lake Erie, January 28, 1970*, p. 4-5.

10. Ibid., p. 9.

11. Ibid., p. 10.

12. Ibid., p. 10-11.

13. The Dominion News, January 29, 1970.

14. National Transportation Safety Board. *Aircraft Accident Report, Apache Airlines, Inc., de Havilland DH-104-7AXC, N4922V, Coolidge, Arizona, May 6, 1971.*

BIBLIOGRAPHY

Angelucci, Enzo. *World Encyclopedia of Civil Aircraft*, Chartwell Books, Edison, New Jersey, 2001.

Cacutt, Len (Editor). *The World's Greatest Aircraft*, Exeter Books, New York, 1988.

Eden, Paul. *Civil Aircraft Today*, Amber Books, London, 2008.

Eden, Paul. *The Encyclopedia of Aircraft of WWII*, Amber Books, London, 2006.

Green, William, Swanborough, Gordon, & Mowinski, John. *Modern Commercial Aircraft*, Portland House, New York, 1987.

Green, William. *The World's Fighting Planes*, Doubleday and Company, Inc., Garden City, New York, 1965.

Gunston, Bill. *American Warplanes*, Crescent Books, New York, 1986.

Holder, Bill & Vadnais, Scott. *The "C" Planes*, Schiffler Publishing Ltd., Atglen, Pennsylvania, 1996.

Mondey, David. *The Illustrated Encyclopedia of Major Airliners of the World*, Aerospace Publishing Ltd., London, 1983.

Munson, Kenneth. *Airliners From 1919 to the Present Day*, Peerage Books, London, 1982.

Munson, Kenneth. *U.S. Commercial Aircraft*, Jane's Publishing Company Limited, London, 1982.

National Aerospace Education Council. *1967 United States Aircraft, Missiles, and Spacecraft*, Washington D. C., 1967.

160

Powers, David G. *Lockheed 188 Electra*, World Transport Press, Inc., Miami, Florida, 1999.

Szurovy, Geza. *Classic American Airliners*, Motorbooks International, St. Paul, Minnesota, 2000.

Taylor, John W. R. & Swanborough, Gordon. *Civil Aircraft of the World*, Ian Allan Ltd., London, 1978.

Taylor, John W. R. & Swanborough, Gordon. *Military Aircraft of the World*, Ian Allen Ltd., London, 1975.

Wilson, Stewart. *Douglas DC-6/7*, Notebook Publications, Bungendore, Australia, 2001.

Winchester, Jim. *American Military Aircraft*, Barnes & Noble Books, New York, 2005.

Winchester, Jim. *Civil Aircraft*, Thunder Bay Press, San Diego, 2004.

Government Reports

Bureau of Air Commerce. *Statement of Probable Cause Concerning an Aircraft Accident which Occurred to a Plane of Northwest Airlines on August 7, 1934 at Milwaukee, Wisconsin*, Department of Commerce, Washington D. C., 1935.

Chernikoff, R. & Ziegler P. N., U.S. Naval Research Laboratory. *An Experimental Evaluation of Four Types of Altimeters Using Both Pilot and Enlisted Men Subjects*, Department of the Navy, Washington D. C., 1964.

Civil Aeronautics Board. *Accident Investigation Report, American Airlines, Inc., Near Buffalo, New York, on January 20, 1954*, Civil Aeronautics

Board, Washington D. C., 1954.

Civil Aeronautics Board. *Accident Investigation Report, Capital Airlines, Inc. and Cessna 140, Milwaukee, Wisconsin, August 7, 1949*, Civil Aeronautics Board, Washington D. C., 1950.

Civil Aeronautics Board. *Accident Investigation Report, Northwest Airlines, Inc., Almelund, Minnesota, October 13, 1950*, Civil Aeronautics Board, Washington D. C., 1951.

Civil Aeronautics Board. *Accident Investigation Report, Trans-Canada Air Lines Viscount, CF-TGR, Flat Rock, Michigan, July 9, 1956*, Civil Aeronautics Board, Washington D. C., 1957.

Civil Aeronautics Board. *Aircraft Accident Investigation Report, Trans World Airlines, Inc., Lockheed Constellation L-1049H, N102R, Midway Airport, Chicago, Illinois, November 24, 1959*, Civil Aeronautics Board, Washington D. C., 1961.

Civil Aeronautics Board. *Aircraft Accident Investigation Report, Northwest Airlines, Inc., Douglas DC-6B, N575, Minneapolis, Minnesota, August 28, 1958*, Civil Aeronautics Board, Washington D. C., 1959.

Knaack, Marcelle Size. *Encyclopedia of U.S. Air Force Aircraft and Missile Systems, Volume II, Post-World War II Bombers, 1945-1973*, Office of Air Force History, United States Air Force, Washington D.C., 1988.

National Transportation Safety Board. *Aircraft Accident Report, United Airlines, Inc., B-727, N7036U, In Lake Michigan, August 16, 1965*, Department of Transportation, Washington D. C., 1967.

National Transportation Safety Board. *Aircraft Accident Report, TAG Airlines, Inc., De Havilland Dove [DH-104], N2300H, In Lake Erie, January 28, 1970, Report# NTSB-AAR-71-5*, U.S. Department of Commerce, Washington D. C., 1971.

National Transportation Safety Board. *Aircraft Accident Report, Allegheny Airlines, Inc., DC-9, N988VJ and a Forth Corporation, Piper PA-28, N7374J, Near Fairland, Indiana, September 9, 1969, Report# NTSB-AAR-70-15*, U.S. Department of Commerce, Washington D. C., 1970.

INDEX